Graphic Algebra

EXPLORATIONS
WITH A
GRAPHING CALCULATOR

D0846164

Gary Asp   John Dowsey   Kaye Stacey   David Tynan

KEY CURRICULUM PRESS
Innovators in Mathematics Education

Editor:	Masha Albrecht
Editorial Assistant:	James A. Browne
Production and Design:	Rhonda Idczak, Idczak Enterprises
Illustration:	Bev Aisbett
Cover Design:	Tom Kurema

| Editorial Director: | John Bergez |
| Publisher: | Steven Rasmussen |

Key Curriculum Press
P.O. Box 2304
Berkeley, CA 94702
(510) 548-2304
editorial@keypress.com
http://www.keypress.com

Curriculum Corporation
P.O. Box 177
Carlton South Vic 3053
Australia

ISBN 1-55953-279-3   10 9 8 7 6 5 4 3 2 1   01 00 99 98 97

Printed in the United States of America

Preface

It is a common saying that "a picture speaks a thousand words." In the study of algebra, the most important pictures are graphs presenting the properties of functions. Although working with graphs has always been recognized as an important way of thinking about mathematical functions, drawing graphs used to be tedious. Drawing just one graph by hand was a major task and students frequently had little energy or time left over to actually use their graphs for anything. The advent of computer and calculator graphing changed this. Now hand-held graphing calculators are becoming commonplace in high school classrooms, and more students have access to function graphing software on a computer.

Graphic Algebra arose from a research project conducted in Australia at the University of Melbourne from 1991 to 1994. The project started with two concerns:

● to improve the teaching of algebra;
● to encourage the use of computers and calculators in the teaching of mathematics.

As a result of this research and classroom piloting, Curriculum Corporation published *Graphic Algebra* in Australia. Subsequently, Key Curriculum Press invited the authors and Curriculum Corporation to collaborate in publishing *Graphic Algebra* so that teachers in the U.S. could benefit from the work and wisdom of their Australian colleagues. We hope you and your students find the results of this collaboration valuable, and look forward to continued collaborations of this kind among math educators internationally.

Gary Asp, John Dowsey, Kaye Stacey, David Tynan

Acknowledgements

Many people have contributed to the success of this project. Anne McLennan and Jo Stephenson, both skilled and experienced teachers, gave us wonderful assistance when we first began to test materials in schools. They were able to assist the teachers and students, all of whom were then unfamiliar with the technology, to get working quickly on the graphing utilities and they suggested many improvements to the examples. During 1994, the project was enormously enriched when David Tynan joined the project team and added his expertise and experience as we prepared the manuscript for publication. A project like this depends on the cooperation and enthusiasm of the students and their teachers who test the material. We extend particular thanks to Barry Hutton, Steve Wright and the students and teachers of Lalor Secondary College, Braemar College and Eltham High School.

Gary Asp, John Dowsey, Kaye Stacey

Project Leaders

Contents

To the Teacher

USING THE BOOK

Graphic Algebra provides teaching materials which address some of the main themes of secondary algebra, explored with either a computer graphing program or a graphing calculator. The materials are intended to enrich the teaching of algebra, to extend students' abilities to work mathematically and to teach students about the use of new technologies. It presents rich teaching episodes that:

● develop student understanding of functions;

● use graphs to teach properties of functions;

● use graphs to solve problems from realistic contexts;

● link different representations so that students learn to move easily between tables of values, algebraic expressions and graphs;

● teach concepts and skills needed for computer or calculator graphing.

The materials have been designed to be used in a variety of ways to supplement and complement the teaching of algebra. The materials assume that students have a basic familiarity with algebraic notation and the Cartesian plane. Other pre-requisite knowledge is noted for each chapter. Teachers can select from the book short or long sequences of work to support teaching from grades 8 to 11 and possibly grade 12.

Because working with a graphing utility often shows familiar ideas in an unfamiliar light, teachers are strongly advised to work through the activities they choose beforehand to realize the full potential of each problem situation.

Structure of the book

There are four chapters that explore particular types of functions—the situations where they commonly arise, their distinguishing properties and the links between their representations as graphs, tables of values and algebraic equations. These chapters are:

Chapter 1:   Linear functions: problems and models

Chapter 2:   Quadratic functions: problems and models

Chapter 4:   Exponential functions: problems and models

Chapter 5:   Reciprocal functions: problems and models

Students can work on these chapters, or a selected part of a chapter, after they have learnt or while they are learning about each particular family of functions.

Two other chapters focus on the issue of scale and the importance of gaining a complete mental picture of the graph of a function. They require a basic familiarity with the specified families of functions, but the materials offer plenty of opportunity to explore graph properties.

These chapters are:

Chapter 3: Scale issues: polynomial functions

Chapter 6: Scale issues: exponential and reciprocal functions

Teachers can work through chapters in sequence or select individual activities for which their students already have an appropriate background.

Individual activities are presented on blackline masters. Answers and extensive teacher notes are also provided.

Teaching styles

The book is intended to supplement or partially replace the teaching of algebra in grades 8 to 11. We appreciate that access to calculators and computers within a school is an ongoing struggle, so we have made it possible to pick and choose tasks of various lengths from within each chapter to suit the time available.

The book supports different styles of teaching. Some parts of the book can be used as an individualized work program. For example, students who are familiar with basic algebraic notation, the Cartesian plane and the basic operation of their calculator or computer could work independently at their own pace on early sections of Chapters 1 and 2, punctuated by teacher intervention and whole class discussion. The time required will depend principally on students' background in equations and graphing.

Some of the problem contexts can be used to introduce new ideas (for example, exponential growth). Alternatively, they offer a novel way to review a topic so that familiar ideas are revisited in a new context. Still other tasks, for example the "transformation creations," may best be set as assignments or projects for students to complete in their own time. These ask students to create interesting designs from graphs, drawing on their artistic ability and mathematical knowledge.

Links with current curriculum documents

Recent curriculum documents such as the National Council of Teachers of Mathematics *Curriculum and Evaluation Standards* and the Australian Education Council's *National Statement on Mathematics in Australian Schools* point to the central place of functions and the use of graphing technology in the core algebra curriculum.

This book attempts to enrich the teaching of algebra by providing interesting problems to be solved using graphing technology. There is no attempt to cover all aspects of the algebra curriculum. However, this book does address the substantial set of learning outcomes in the following list. The topics under the headings Algebra and Functions have been specified by the *NCTM Standards* to receive increased attention in math classrooms.

Algebra:
- using real-world problems to motivate and apply theory;
- using computer utilities to develop conceptual understanding.

Functions:

- expressing function equations in standardized forms as checks on the reasonableness of graphs produced by graphing utilities;
- constructing functions as models of real-world problems;
- making connections between a problem situation, its model as a function in symbolic form, and the graph of that function.

Some more specific skills developed in this book include:

- recognizing and representing linear, reciprocal, quadratic, polynomial and exponential functions in tables, symbols and graphs and identifying the assumptions involved in using these functions as models;
- drawing lines of best fit by eye, and interpolating and extrapolating sensibly.

CHOOSING AND USING A GRAPHING UTILITY

Software and hardware

The activities in this book require only the facilities that are currently available on all good quality graphing utilities. The intention is that with minimal adaptation, teachers will be able to use any of the graphing utilities commonly available in schools. At the time of writing, appropriate facilities are available on the following calculators and software as well as many others.

Examples of suitable calculators:

- Texas Instruments TI-83, TI-82, TI-80
- Casio CFX-9850G, CFX-7400G
- Sharp® EL-9600, EL-9300
- Hewlett-Packard® 38G, 48G

Examples of suitable software:

- Most symbolic algebra packages such as *Derive®*, *Mathematica®* and *Mathcad*
- GrafEq™, produced by Pedagoguery Software

The graphing utility on a spreadsheet or statistics program is not suitable.

In order to assist teachers and students who are not yet very familiar with the basic working of a graphing calculator, the teacher notes and appendices provide detailed instructions for working through the materials with three of the currently popular, affordable and capable graphing calculators.

Instructions are given for these three graphing calculators in the appendices:

- Graphing calculator TI-82/83, available from retailers of Texas Instruments calculators.
- Graphing calculator CFX-9850G, available from retailers of Casio calculators.
- Graphing calculator HP38G, available from retailers of Hewlett-Packard calculators.

The book provides appendices which give easy instructions for these graphing utilities. They are not product manuals, but rather a collection of "How to ..." descriptions of the procedures that are needed to complete all tasks within this book. Teachers are strongly advised to familiarize themselves with all the features of the graphing utility in the relevant appendix.

The availability of graphing utilities is increasing rapidly so the price is likely to decrease further and new models will be introduced. Therefore, we have, as far as possible, written activities which are not machine dependent.

Computers or calculators?

Is it better to use computers or calculators for function graphing? The rapid increase in the sophistication, affordability and ease of use of graphing calculators promises to improve dramatically the accessibility of graphing utilities for mathematics teachers and students. The portability of calculators also lessens the common separation of the mathematics classroom from the location of useful technology-rich tools.

On the other hand, computer graphing utilities have impressive resolution, fantastic color, excellent printing capabilities. Soon, laptop and palmtop computers may be as accessible and portable as calculators are now. We hope that many students who are introduced to one graphing utility will understand the basic principles and be able to move flexibly to others.

TEACHING CONCERNS

Teacher notes

Teacher notes are found in Appendix A. They have a number of purposes which include:
- providing assistance in using the graphing utilities;
- drawing attention to common difficulties encountered by students;
- giving additional information about the problems and answers;
- giving hints for teaching arising from the field tests of the materials.

The need for explicit teaching

When teachers first field tested the project materials, many of them had great difficulty securing adequate time in the computer laboratory. Perhaps for this reason, they tended to let students work individually or in pairs, with minimal time with the whole class together. We found that students worked through the examples successfully, but many of them did not learn as well as they might. What was missing was the teacher's perspective: pointing out what is important, asking challenging questions, discussing and emphasizing key points with all the class.

All these teaching behaviors help students reflect on the work that they are doing and it is from this reflection that learning occurs. We don't learn just by doing, but by reflecting on what we do. The "Teacher notes" indicate some of these points.

Understanding scaling and zooming

Our research, and that of our colleagues at the University of Melbourne, has demonstrated that issues of scale are critical for students' understanding of graphs. The strength of graphing utilities is the total flexibility of scaling that is available. Almost at the press of a button, we can see any part of the graph with any scale. For students drawing graphs by hand, deciding on an appropriate scale for a graph is a major hurdle. However, with a graphing utility the initial choice of scale is not important and experimenting is easy, although interpreting the results can be tricky.

Many students, particularly when using graphing utilities, misinterpret graphs by not appreciating that there are many "views" of a graph, and that zooming both in and out is sometimes necessary to get a complete picture of the behavior of a function. To solve problems with graphs of functions, students need to have a good idea of the big picture of a graph, not just what can be seen through any one viewing window. Consequently, there are two chapters (3 and 6) looking at functions both globally and locally. These chapters confront student misconceptions about scale in the context of function graphing.

Each of these chapters is broken into two sections:

- **the big picture** which emphasizes the importance of zooming out and in to get a good understanding of what the function looks like;

- **the rubber sheet** which draws attention to what effect scale can have on the appearance of a graph.

Quantities on the axes

One of the difficulties of using graphing utilities is that it is not easy (and on some graphing utilities not possible) to label the axes. This is a disadvantage, as students must keep in mind exactly what variables they have plotted on each axis. In the "Lemon and lime" problem (Chapter 1), for example, on one axis students have the number of dollars that they have taken, and on the other they have the number of dollars of profit. To use the graph, they need to keep these two quantities firmly in mind. Teachers testing the material noticed that students found this difficult, but when they succeeded they seemed to have a greater appreciation of the importance of knowing precisely what the variable is on each axis. We recommend that students begin each problem by making a quick sketch of the graph as it appears in the viewing window and labeling the axes fully. Where there is more than one graph in the view, each graph should be clearly labeled.

Labeling carefully may help students avoid classic mistakes such as interpreting the travel graph shown as a trip to the north-east, then the south-east or as a journey over a mountain.

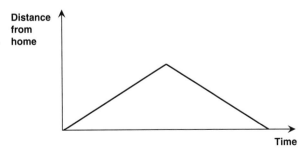

Pre-requisite knowledge and skills

Before they commence the activities in this book, students should have had some experience with algebraic variables in a variety of contexts. It is assumed that students will be familiar with the Cartesian plane and will have had some experience of plotting graphs of simple linear functions by hand. A detailed description of the pre-requisite knowledge for each chapter is given below.

Research on students' difficulties with beginning graphing indicates that teachers need to emphasize the following skills:

- reading points which do not have labeled coordinates;
- reading points which are not on the grid;
- reading information about intervals between points, not just points.

During the research project, we found evidence that students benefited from doing some plotting of points by hand. Otherwise some students will rely on the "show coordinates" facility of the graphing utility and never practice the skill themselves sufficiently for long-term retention.

Assumed knowledge

Chapter 1:

- understanding of linear expressions such as $2x - 3$;
- calculating tables of values from linear rules;
- plotting straight line graphs by hand on a Cartesian plane;
- operating at a basic level with the computer or calculator and printer.

Chapter 2:

- understanding of quadratic expressions such as $x^2 + 2x - 3$;
- dealing with functions by hand, for example calculating tables of values, plotting graphs by hand on a Cartesian plane, interpreting the meaning of points on graphs;
- operating a graphing utility at a basic level, for example graphing, reading coordinates, zooming, clearing, finding points of intersection, changing the viewing window;
- using function notation ($F(x) = \ldots$).

Chapter 3:

- reading polynomial expressions such as $x^4 + 2x - 3$;
- assumed knowledge as for Chapter 2 above.

Chapter 4:

- understanding of exponential notation, for example, 10^3, and being able to read numbers written in scientific notation;
- assumed knowledge as for Chapter 2 above.

Chapter 5:
- being able to change the subject of a formula, for example, going from:
  $xy = 30$ to $y = \dfrac{30}{x}$ and rearranging expressions such as $3 + \dfrac{14}{2x} - 5$;
- assumed knowledge as for Chapter 2 above.

Chapter 6:
- understanding of polynomial, exponential and reciprocal expressions;
- assumed knowledge as for Chapter 2 above.

WHY ARE FUNCTION CONCEPTS IMPORTANT?

Algebra at school has many different facets, including finding unknown numbers, expressing general properties of numbers and studying the behavior of functions. The approach to algebra adopted in this book is oriented to functions in a number of ways.

A functions approach

The functions approach is evident in the way in which solving equations is presented and in the applications which are used to develop the concepts involved. For example, in the "Lemon and lime" problem (Chapter 1) students are effectively solving simultaneous equations. Students look at the profit to be made by selling various quantities of lemonade and then pick the break-even point rather than focusing solely on the break-even point via an algebraic solution. Problems ask students to give a range of possibilities when something happens rather than to find a solution in one particular instance.

Studying the properties of functions

An understanding of the way in which families of functions behave is an important goal of learning algebra and an important objective of this book. It is intended that students will get a good understanding of the type of situations where a particular family of functions is likely to be relevant. For example, they should come to recognize that if a given change in one variable produces a constant change in the other, a linear function is likely to describe the relationship. On the other hand, if a constant change in one variable gives a constant percentage change in the other, an exponential function will describe the behavior. Graphing software lets students easily experiment with a variety of examples from which they can build an intuitive understanding of functional behavior.

Moving between representations

Mathematical relationships between variables can usually be presented in tables of values, as formulas and as graphs. This book aims to develop in students the ability to move confidently between these representations, so that they can bring formal algebraic manipulative skills and skills of graphical interpretation to bear on the one problem.

Function notation

An obvious feature of the book is the use of function notation from the start. For example, we write $P(x) = 2x - 3$ rather than $y = 2x - 3$ in the first section. This notation is used in higher mathematics and it is used by several, but not all, common graphing utilities. Some graphing utilities in common use require function notation, others require all functions to be entered as $y =$ (some expression in x), others require different functions to be called Y_1 or Y_2, Y_3, etc. Some permit a variety of letters to be used, others only allow x and y. Because this book is written for a variety of graphing utilities, teachers will need to help students translate between notations. Indeed, this is an important ability required for learning to use graphing utilities. Students need to be able to translate the notation used in a question into the appropriate symbolism for their own machine. Our field testing showed that students adapted readily to function notation, with no substantial difficulties.

1 Linear functions: problems and models

EXPLORING LINEAR RELATIONSHIPS

Lemonade

Angela makes some lemonade to sell at a school party. She plans to sell drinks in paper cups containing 100 milliliters of lemonade. She will charge 20 cents for each drink.

1 How much money will she receive if she sells:

    a 45 drinks? _____   **b** 6.5 liters? _____

Angela spent $3.00 buying the ingredients for her lemonade. She got some things for no cost, such as lots of lemons from her neighbor's lemon tree.

2 How much profit will she make if she sells:

    a 45 drinks? _____   **b** 6.5 liters? _____

How does the profit change with the number of liters of lemonade sold? Let x be the number of liters sold and let $P(x)$ be the profit in dollars. Let us find a rule for $P(x)$.

3 a How many dollars does Angela collect for each liter that she sells? _____

    b If she sells x liters, how many dollars will she collect? _____

    c If she spent $3.00 on ingredients,
    write the rule that describes her profit $P(x)$. _____

Let us now draw a graph of $P(x)$, the profit function. It will tell us how the profit changes with the number of liters of lemonade she sells.

4 Complete the following table by finding the value of $P(x)$ for the values for x in the table. One value has been done for you.

x	0	1	2	3	4	5
$P(x)$		−1				

Plot the pairs of values on the following graph. You should find that the points lie on a straight line.

Use your ruler to draw the straight line (extend it beyond the last points).

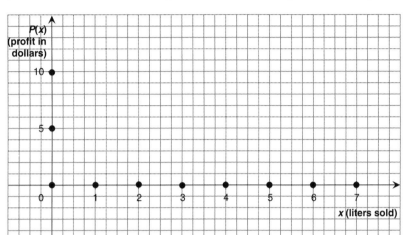

Your graph of $P(x)$ shows how Angela's profit increases as the number of liters of lemonade sold increases. It gives a useful *picture* of the profit function.

5 Use your straight line graph to answer the following questions.

a What will Angela's profit be if she sells 6 liters of lemonade? _____

b If Angela's profit is $4.00, how many liters would she have sold? _____
How many drinks is this? _____

c What will Angela's profit be if she sells 70 drinks of lemonade? _____

d In one part of the graph, $P(x)$ has negative values. What does this mean?

_____

Lemonade with a graphing utility

In the lemonade problem we used a rule for Angela's profit to help draw a graph of the profit function. Drawing graphs accurately like this is time consuming—we are now going to use a graphing utility to do some of the hard work for us.

Let us look at the lemonade problem again, this time with the aid of a graphing utility. The sequence of steps illustrated in the box below describes how to enter a function and plot its graph using a graphing utility.

A QUICK START TO USING A GRAPHING UTILITY

1 Create a blank screen with your graphing utility.

2 Ensure that you have started with the default viewing window.

3 Enter the rule for Angela's profit function $P(x) = 2x - 3$.

4 Plot the graph of this function.

5 Ensure that the cursor coordinates in the graph window are displayed.

We are now going to use the graph of the function to answer some of the questions we looked at earlier. By moving the cursor (or pointer) about the screen, we can find the coordinates of the point where the cursor is located. This idea is used in the following question.

1 a To find the profit for $x = 2$, position your cursor on the graph as near to $x = 2$ as you can. Write down the value of $P(2)$ that you get. _____.

How close is this value to the value in the table you prepared earlier? _____

Complete using the information read from the graph:

$P(2) =$ _____, therefore if Angela sells _____ liters of lemonade, her profit will be approximately _____.

b i From the graph, write down an estimate of Angela's profit if she sells 2.6 liters of lemonade. _____

ii Check this result with the rule $P(x) = 2x - 3$. _____

c i From the graph, how many liters of lemonade will Angela have to sell to just break even (that is, when the profit is zero)? _____

ii Check this result with the rule for $P(x)$. _____

d Reading from the graph determine what will happen if Angela only sells 1 liter of lemonade. _____

e i If Angela makes a profit of $2.00, read from the graph how many liters she has sold. _____

ii Check this result with the rule for $P(x)$. _____

f i Repeat part **e** if Angela makes a profit of $3.80. _____

ii Check this result with the rule for $P(x)$. _____

One of the main advantages of a graphing utility is that we can quickly change the viewing window. We can zoom out to see more of the graph or we can zoom in to focus on a small part of the graph. If you haven't zoomed yet, you will need to in the next question.

2 a i Zoom out to get an appropriate viewing window which shows the profit Angela makes if she sells 22 liters of lemonade.

Write down the dimensions of the viewing window. _____

From the graph, what profit does Angela make? _____

ii Check this result with the rule for $P(x)$. _____

b i How many liters would Angela have to sell to make a profit of $7.80? More accurate answers can be found from the graph if you zoom in around the point you want.
Zoom in to find the answer accurately. _____

ii Check this result with the rule for $P(x)$. _____

c i Angela's ingredients were enough to make 30 liters of lemonade. If she sells all of it, how much profit does she make? Use a combination of zooming out and zooming in to answer this question as accurately as you can. _____

ii Check this result with the rule for $P(x)$. _____

Lemon and lime

Angela's best friend Kate is going to join Angela's drinks stall. She makes lime fizz with fresh limes from her lime tree and other special ingredients. She plans to charge 25 cents per 100 milliliter drink. Her ingredients cost $5.00.

1 Complete the following sentences.

For each liter of lime fizz that Kate sells, she receives $_____, so if she sells x liters, now she receives $_____.
Since she spent $5.00 on ingredients, her profit $Q(x)$, in dollars, is given by the rule $Q(x) = $_____.

Let us look at a graph of both Angela's and Kate's profit functions. You will have to plot two lines on one set of axes.

2 Using the default window, enter and plot both Angela's and Kate's profit functions—that is $P(x) = 2x - 3$ and $Q(x) = 2.5x - 5$. Zoom out, if necessary, until you see two straight line graphs and their point of intersection. Draw a quick sketch graph of what you see. Label each graph.

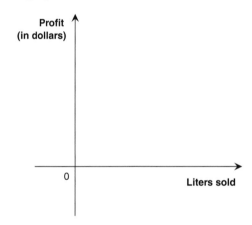

3 Use the graph (and then the rule) to answer these questions. To get accurate answers, you need to change the viewing window (for example, by zooming out and then zooming in, or by setting the window dimensions).

a i Estimate how much profit Kate will make if she sells 2.6 liters of lime fizz. _____

ii Check this result with the rule for $Q(x)$. _____

b i How many liters of lime fizz will Kate have to sell to just break even (remember, this is when the profit is zero)? _____

ii Check this result with the rule for $Q(x)$. _____

c i If Kate makes a profit of $4.00, how many liters of lime fizz has she sold? _____

ii Check this result with the rule for $Q(x)$. _____

d i If Kate makes a profit of $4.75, how many liters of lime fizz has she sold? _____

ii Check this result with the rule for $Q(x)$. _____

4 Using both graphs, answer the following questions.

   a i If Angela and Kate each sell 3 liters of lemonade and lime fizz respectively, who makes the most profit, and by how much? _____ _____

   ii Check your answer with the rules for $P(x)$ and $Q(x)$.

   _____

   _____

   b i If Angela and Kate each sell 7 liters of lemonade and lime fizz respectively, who makes the most profit, and by how much? _____ _____

   ii Check your answer with the rules for $P(x)$ and $Q(x)$.

   _____

   _____

   c i If Angela and Kate each want $10.00 profit, who has to sell the most drink? _____

   ii How many extra liters does she sell? _____

   iii Check your answer with the rules for $P(x)$ and $Q(x)$.

   _____

   _____

   _____

5 The graphs for $P(x)$ and $Q(x)$ intersect at a point.

   a Find the coordinates of the point where they intersect as accurately as you can. (____, ____)

   b What does the first number in the coordinate pair represent?

   _____

   c What does the second number in the coordinate pair represent?

   _____

Rohan and Effie

Rohan and Effie also join the drinks stall. Suppose Rohan's ingredients for lemonade cost $4.00 and he decides to charge 25 cents per drink. Then his price per liter (1 liter = 10 drinks) will be $2.50. The rule for his profit function $S(x)$, where $S(x)$ is the profit in dollars and x is the number of liters sold, is:

$$S(x) = 2.5x - 4$$

1 Suppose Effie pays $7.00 for ingredients for lime fizz and she decides to charge 30 cents per drink. What is the rule for Effie's profit function $T(x)$, where $T(x)$ is the profit in dollars and x is the number of liters sold? _____

Using your graphing utility, enter and plot the profit functions $S(x)$ and $T(x)$.

2 Answer the following questions using the new graphs. Zoom in and out to find the answer correct to the nearest cent or 100 milliliters (0.1 liters).

a How many liters of lemonade would Rohan have to sell to break even? _____

b How many liters of lime fizz would Effie have to sell to break even? _____

c i If Rohan and Effie each sell 3.5 liters of lemonade and lime fizz respectively, who makes the most profit, and by how much? _____ _____

    ii Check using the appropriate rules for the two profit functions.

    _____

    _____

d i If Rohan and Effie each sell 8 liters of lemonade and lime fizz respectively, who makes the most profit, and by how much? _____ _____

    ii Check using the rules for the two profit functions.

    _____

    _____

e i If Rohan and Effie each make $14.00 profit, who sells the most drink, and by how much? _____ _____

    ii Check using the rules.

    _____

    _____

    _____

3 The graphs for $S(x)$ and $T(x)$ intersect at a point.

a Find the coordinates of this point as accurately as you can.(____, ____)

b What does the first number in the coordinate pair represent?

    _____

c What does the second number in the coordinate pair represent?

    _____

Mobile phone charges

OZ-Mobile is a newly launched mobile phone network provider who will offer good charging rates to attract customers from its competitors. Customers can choose from three different charging schemes.

OZ-Mobile Scheme *A*—$10 rental per month and a call charge of $1.20 per minute.

OZ-Mobile Scheme *B*—$20 rental per month and a call charge of $0.80 per minute.

OZ-Mobile Scheme *C*—$35 rental per month and a call charge of $0.40 per minute.

To make the problem simpler, assume that if you use part of a minute you are charged for part of a minute.

1 Complete the following table for cost estimates for each scheme for one month, determining the most expensive and least expensive.

Call time	Cost for Scheme A	Cost for Scheme B	Cost for Scheme C	Most expensive	Least expensive
20 minutes	$34.00	$36.00	$43.00	C	A
30 minutes					
40 minutes					
50 minutes					

Let $A(m)$, $B(m)$ and $C(m)$ be the monthly cost functions in dollars for each of the schemes where m represents the number of minutes that the caller has been on-line during that month.

2 Write down the rules for $A(m)$, $B(m)$ and $C(m)$.

_____

3 Create a blank screen with your graphing utility. Plot each of the three cost functions on the same set of axes.

  a Adjust the viewing window to show all three lines and their points of intersection. Draw a quick sketch graph of what you see in the viewing window. Label the axes and lines appropriately.

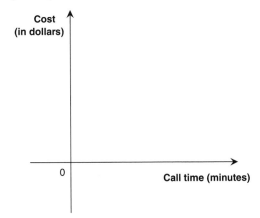

  b Find the coordinates of the points at which the graphs intersect. Label these on your sketch. What do these points represent?

_____

_____

4 On a separate sheet, write a brief report explaining which scheme will be best for different customers, based upon the number of minutes that they might be on-line in a month. Your report should indicate when Scheme A is best, when Scheme B is best, and when Scheme C is best.

FITTING LINEAR FUNCTIONS TO DATA

Arm span versus height

It has been suggested that a linear relationship exists between the height of a person and their arm span. First we will collect some data on heights and arm spans. Then we will try some linear rules to see how well they fit the data.

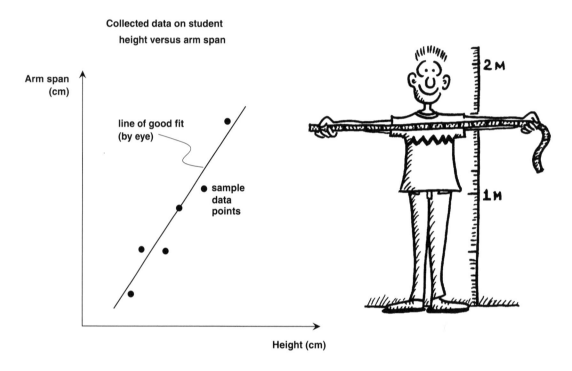

A sample graph showing the relationship of data collected on student height and arm span is shown above.

Measure the heights and arm spans (fingertip to fingertip) of 10 students. Try to choose students of different heights, so that the points will be reasonably well spaced.

1 When you have collected the data, complete the first two rows in the following table.

Height in cm (h)										
Arm span in cm (A)										
Predicted arm span										
Difference in measured and predicted value										

Using your graphing utility, enter and plot the data.

Rebecca claims that a person's arm span is roughly equal to the person's height. So Rebecca thinks that the linear rule $A = h$ will be a good fit. Let us test Rebecca's claim.

2 Plot Rebecca's rule $A = h$, where h is student height in centimeters and A is student arm span in centimeters.

Your graph may look like the diagram below which shows data from Happy Valley High School and the graph of the line $A = h$.

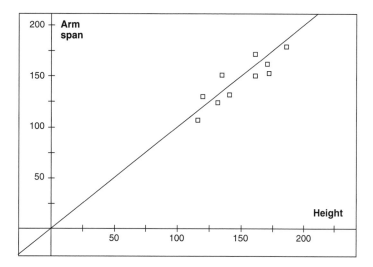

a Are your points "close to the line" $A = h$? _____

b How many of your points lie on each side of the line? _____

c Do the points above the line seem to be spread out like the points below the

line? _____

3 To find a new rule that is better than Rebecca's rule, plot different linear rules of the form $A = $ ___ $h + $ ___. Re-apply the criteria used above to find by eye what appears to be a good fit. Complete the following sentence.

The relationship between arm span (A) and height (h) is well described by:

$$A = \underline{\quad} h + \underline{\quad}$$

It would be useful to test how well your rule fits your sample measurements.

4 a For each height, find the arm span given by your rule. This is called the "predicted" arm span. It may be different from the measured arm span. Enter the predicted arm spans in the third row of the table on the previous page.

b In the fourth row, enter the difference between a student's measured arm span and the predicted arm span. Use the size of the difference only, not whether the difference is positive or negative.

As a rough guide to how well your rule fits, an *average difference* can be calculated.

5 a Add the 10 differences (last row) from the table that you have created. This will give you the total difference. _____

b Calculate the average difference by dividing the total difference by the number of students in the sample (10 in this case). _____

9

6 a Use the method of questions 4 and 5 to calculate
the average difference for Rebecca's rule. _____

b The lower the average difference, the better the rule fits the data.
Which rule, yours or Rebecca's, fits the data better? _____

7 Choose the better of the two rules, yours or Rebecca's. Gather data for a new sample
of 10 students. Plot this data and the rule you have chosen using your graphing utility.

a Judging by eye, does the line appear to fit the data well? Give reasons.

_____

_____

b Complete the table below.

c Calculate the average difference for this new sample. _____

d Compare the average difference for this new sample with the average difference for
the original sample. If they are different, explain why this is the case.

_____

_____

Height in cm (*h*)									
Arm span in cm (*A*)									
Predicted arm span									
Difference between measured value and predicted value									

International shoe sizes

When we buy shoes, we usually know which shoe size is best for us. However, sometimes shoes
of the same size have different numbers marked on the sole. Countries such as France, the
United Kingdom, Japan and the United States all employ different systems of shoe sizes.

The original British rule for determining shoe sizes is described by the principle:

When a foot grows $\frac{1}{6}$ inch, a person requires another $\frac{1}{2}$ size in shoe.

This can also be read as:

For an increase of 1 inch in the shoe length, the shoe size will increase 3 sizes.

The shoe sizes start at 1 for the smallest normal foot (about $8\frac{1}{2}$ inches long). From this, a rule
which calculates the British shoe size *S* based on the shoe length *L*, in inches, is given by:

$$S = 3L - 25, \text{ where } L \text{ is in inches}$$

So, a shoe length of 9 inches would give a shoe size of 2, since $S = 3 \times 9 - 25 = 2$ and a shoe
length of 10 inches would give a shoe size of 5, since $S = 3 \times 10 - 25 = 5$. This shows that an
increase of 1 inch gives an increase of 3 sizes.

Most countries have now switched to metric measurements, and the rule can be adjusted as follows:

● an increase of 1 inch in the shoe length increases the shoe size by 3 sizes
  (in metric, an increase of 2.54 cm increases the shoe size by 3 sizes);

● an increase of 1 cm in the shoe length increases the shoe size by $\frac{3}{2.54}$ or approximately 1.18 sizes *(an increase of 1 cm increases the shoe size by just over 1 size);*

● an increase of 1 mm increases the shoe size by $\frac{1.18}{10}$ or approximately 0.118 sizes
  (an increase of 1 mm increases the shoe size by just over a tenth of a size).

Therefore, the rule which calculates the British shoe size S based on the shoe length L in millimeters is:

$$S = 0.118L - 25$$

The table below is copied from the British manufacturers' shoe size comparison chart, and shows the lengths of shoes of different sizes.

Shoe length (nearest mm)	220	224	229	233	237	241	246	250	254	258	263	267	271
British shoe size	1	$1\frac{1}{2}$	2	$2\frac{1}{2}$	3	$3\frac{1}{2}$	4	$4\frac{1}{2}$	5	$5\frac{1}{2}$	6	$6\frac{1}{2}$	7

1 a To check that the rule in metric works, we will test it on the first data point in the table (220 mm, shoe size 1). Complete the following sentence.

From the rule $S = 0.118 (220) - 25 =$ _____

Therefore $S =$ _____ (round to nearest whole number or half)

b Repeat part **a** for the data point $(233, 2\frac{1}{2})$. _____

Using your graphing utility, enter the function rule $S = 0.118L - 25$ and plot its graph.

Change the viewing window so that it shows shoe lengths from about 200 mm to 320 mm and shoe sizes up to 11.

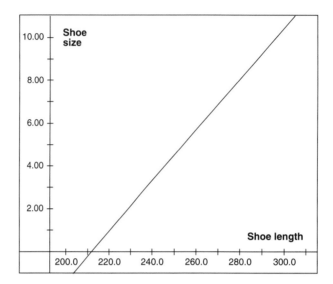

Use the graph to answer the following questions.

2 What British shoe size corresponds to a shoe length of 280 mm? _____

3 What would be the length to the nearest millimeter of a shoe that has a British shoe size of 9? _____

4 Suppose a British manufacturer makes a shoe with a shoe length of 256 mm. What shoe size should the manufacturer mark on the sole? Explain your answer.

_____

_____

There are conversion tables that show equivalent United States (US) men's, US women's, and French shoe sizes for a given British shoe size. Here is part of such a table.

Shoe length (nearest mm)	220	224	229	233	237	241	246	250	254	258	263	267	271
British shoe size	1	$1\frac{1}{2}$	2	$2\frac{1}{2}$	3	$3\frac{1}{2}$	4	$4\frac{1}{2}$	5	$5\frac{1}{2}$	6	$6\frac{1}{2}$	7
US men's shoe size	2	$2\frac{1}{2}$	3	$3\frac{1}{2}$	4	$4\frac{1}{2}$	5	$5\frac{1}{2}$	6	$6\frac{1}{2}$	7	$7\frac{1}{2}$	8
US women's shoe size	4	$4\frac{1}{2}$	5	$5\frac{1}{2}$	6	$6\frac{1}{2}$	7	$7\frac{1}{2}$	8	$8\frac{1}{2}$	9	$9\frac{1}{2}$	10

5 What is the relationship between British shoe size and US men's shoe size?

_____

6 a Complete the following to find a rule relating US men's shoe size to shoe length in millimeters.

    For British shoe sizes $S = 0.118L - 25$

    So for US men's shoe sizes $S = \underline{\hspace{1cm}} L - \underline{\hspace{1cm}}$

  b Substitute in the values 220 mm and US men's shoe size 2 to test your rule.

On the same set of axes as before, enter and plot a function on your graphing utility for US men's shoe size in terms of shoe length.

7 Look at the two graphs on the screen (British and US men's). What is the relationship between the lines? Why does this relationship exist?

Now, on the same set of axes, enter and plot a function for the US women's shoe size in terms of the shoe length.

8 What is the relationship between US men's shoe size and US women's shoe size?

9 a Complete the following to find a rule relating US women's shoe size to the shoe length in millimeters.

    For US men's shoe sizes $S = \underline{\hspace{1cm}} L - \underline{\hspace{1cm}}$

    For US women's shoe sizes $S = \underline{\hspace{1cm}} L - \underline{\hspace{1cm}}$

  b Test your rule with the point (220 mm, US women's shoe size 4).

10 Measure your own shoe length with a ruler. Using the three graphs displayed on your graphing utility, work out the shoe size you should be for each measurement system.

11 Read the size marked on your shoe and decide which, if any, of the three measurement systems was used to mark your shoe?

The size on your shoe could come from a different shoe measurement system. It could be the "continental" shoe measurement system. The table shown below is from the manufacturers.

Shoe length (mm)	220	227	233	240	247	253	260	267	273
Continental shoe size	33	34	35	36	37	38	39	40	41

Using your graphing utility, enter and and plot the data for the continental shoe size system shown in the table above.

12 Examine the table carefully to see how the change in shoe length changes the shoe size. Use this to help "fit" a line to the data. When you have found a line of good fit by eye, write down the rule for your straight line.

For continental shoe size:

$$S = \underline{\hspace{1cm}} L - \underline{\hspace{1cm}}$$

13 We can restate the above rule in two ways.

a An increase of 1 mm in the shoe length increases the continental shoe size by about _____.

b An increase of about _____ mm in the shoe length increases the continental shoe size by 1.

Some graphing utilities can create a table of values. Others may only give you one value at a time.

14 By creating a table or calculating the values one at a time write down the shoe sizes that correspond to shoe lengths of:

a 240 mm _____ **b** 247 mm _____

c 253 mm _____ **d** 260 mm _____

Comment on how well these values match those given in the continental manufacturers' table.

_____

_____

TRANSFORMATION CREATIONS ON FAMILIES OF LINEAR FUNCTIONS

Creations

A graphing utility can be used to create patterns. The following exercises challenge you to create patterns using the graphs of linear functions.

Write down the functions that you use. The creations do not need to be exactly the same as the ones shown, but the picture you make should look similar. It will help if you set the viewing window for each creation before you start.

1 Rain

Adjust the viewing window so that you are looking at the region bounded by:

$$-4 \leq x \leq 4 \text{ and } -3 \leq y \leq 3$$

Enter and plot functions to draw sheets of rain like the ones shown. Notice that all lines are parallel and the points of intersection on the x-axis are equally spaced.

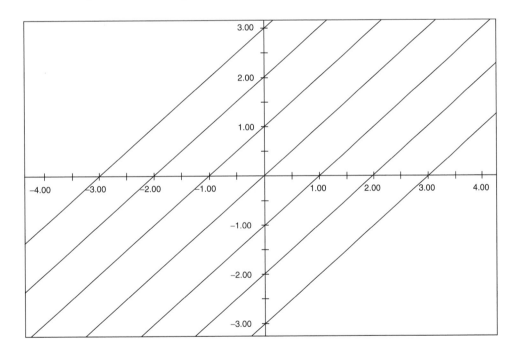

Record the functions that you have used below.

_____

_____

_____

What do you notice about the functions that create this pattern?

_____

2 Horizon

Adjust the viewing window so that you are looking at the region bounded by:

$$-4 \le x \le 4 \text{ and } -1 \le y \le 5$$

Horizon is a series of lines, parallel to the x-axis. Create a pattern the same or similar to the one shown here.

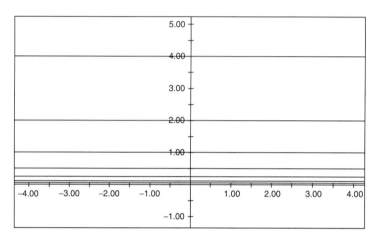

Record the functions that you have used to the right of the graph above.

What do you notice about the functions that create this pattern?

3 Triangle

Adjust the viewing window so that you are looking at the region bounded by:

$$-7 \le x \le 7 \text{ and } -12 \le y \le 16$$

Graph three lines so that they create a triangle similar, but not necessarily identical, to the one shown below.

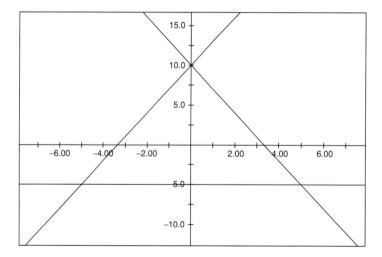

Record the functions that you have used to the right of the graph above.

What do you notice about the functions that create this pattern?

4 Diamonds

Adjust the viewing window so that you are looking at the region bounded by:
$$-3 \le x \le 3 \text{ and } -4 \le y \le 4$$
A diamond pattern can be created by two sets of parallel lines crossing each other. Create a pattern similar to the one shown below. Notice the similarities to the rain pattern on page 15. Again the points of intersection on the x-axis are equally spaced.

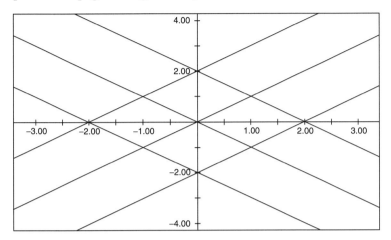

Record the functions that you have used to the right of the graph above.

What do you notice about the functions that create this pattern?

5 Windmill

Adjust the viewing window so that you are looking at the region bounded by:
$$-16 \le x \le 16 \text{ and } -16 \le y \le 16$$
Windmills often have four equally spaced blades. Two lines need to be symmetrical around the x-axis and two lines need to be symmetrical around the y-axis.

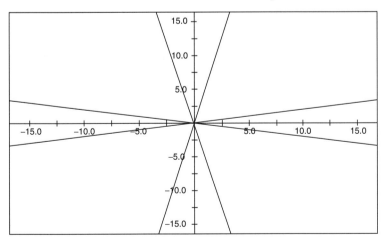

Record the functions that you have used to the right of the graph above.

What do you notice about the functions that create this pattern?

6 Sparkler

Adjust the viewing window so that you are looking at the region bounded by:

$$-1 \le x \le 11 \text{ and } -1 \le y \le 11$$

A sparkler pattern can be created by lines intersecting at one point. Create a pattern of lines that intersect at the point $(5, 5)$, like the one shown.

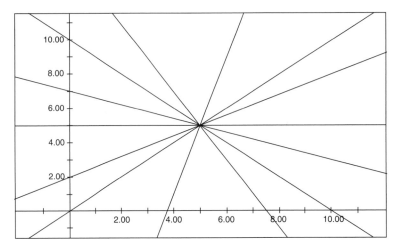

Record the functions that you have used to the right of the graph above.

7 Create your own design

Make up a creation of your own, using linear function rules.

On another sheet of paper sketch your creation. List the functions you used and name the creation.

Linear function graphs and constants

For linear functions the general rule is of the form:

$$y = ax + b$$

By working through the seven "creations" you will have noticed how the graphs change when you change a and b. Use this knowledge to answer the next questions. You may have to experiment further to answer the questions.

1 Complete the following sentences to describe the effect of the constant a on the graph of a linear function.

   a If a is positive then _____

   b If a is negative then _____

   c If a is large and positive then _____

   d If a is small and positive then _____

2 Complete the following sentences to describe the effect of the constant b on the graph of a linear function.

   a If b is positive then _____

    b If b is negative then _____

    c If b is near zero then _____

  3 If two or more lines are parallel, what can you say about their values of a or b?

_____

Transformation creations with restrictions

Sometimes formulas only make sense over a "restricted domain." For example, in the "lemonade" case, x is the number of liters of drink sold and cannot be negative, as shown on the graph below.

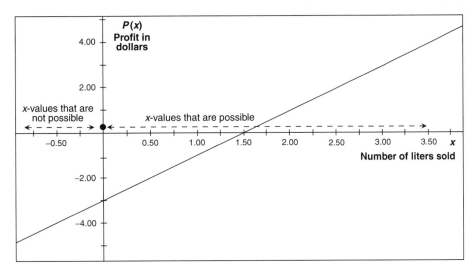

So in the "lemonade" example, Angela's profit function is better defined as:

$$P(x) = 2x - 3 \text{ for } x \geq 0$$

Most graphing utilities allow you to enter rules with restrictions. When this is done for Angela's profit function, the graph changes to this.

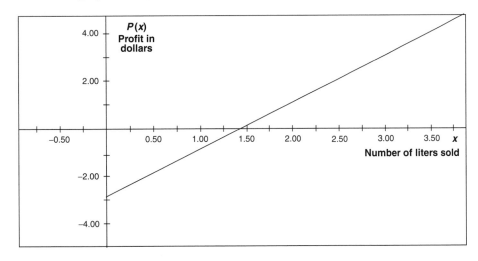

In the following creations, some of the rules entered need to include a restriction on the domain, for example, to include only positive values of x. These conditions restrict the domain of $f(x)$.

1 Mountains

Adjust the viewing window so that you are looking at the region bounded by:
$$-5 \leq x \leq 5 \text{ and } -5 \leq y \leq 5$$
Create a series of mountain peaks similar to those shown.

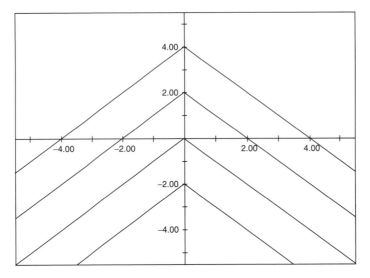

Hint: Place restrictions on the values that x can take, and define eight separate functions.

Record the functions that you have used and their restrictions to the right of the graph.

2 Peaks

Adjust the viewing window so that you are looking at the region bounded by:
$$-5 \leq x \leq 5 \text{ and } -10 \leq y \leq 17$$
Create a series of peaks, similar to those shown.

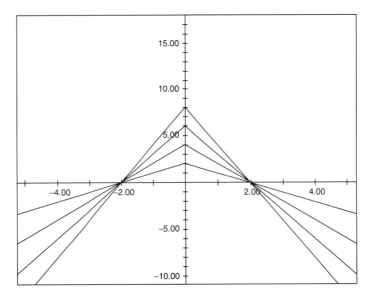

Hint: Restrictions are placed on the values that x can take.

Record the functions that you have used and their restrictions to the right of the graph.

3 Triangle

Adjust the viewing window so that you are looking at the region bounded by:

$$-7 \leq x \leq 7 \text{ and } -11 \leq y \leq 16$$

Draw a triangle with vertices at the points $(0, 10)$, $(5, -5)$ and $(-5, -5)$.

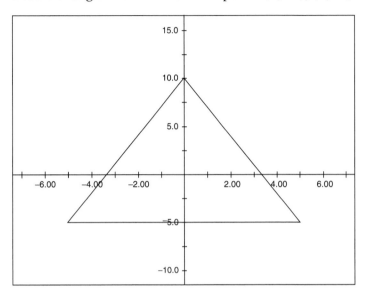

Record the functions that you have used and their restrictions to the right of the graph.

4 Star

Adjust the viewing window so that you are looking at the region bounded by:

$$-7 \leq x \leq 7 \text{ and } -11 \leq y \leq 16$$

Draw a star similar to the one shown.

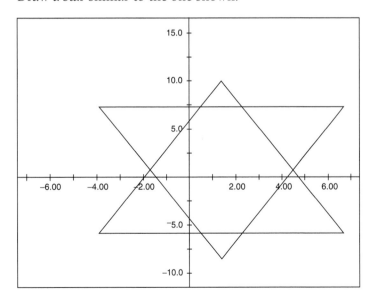

Record the functions that you have used and their restrictions to the right of the graph.

Hint: Use your triangle from the Triangle creation.

2 Quadratic functions: problems and models

EXPLORING QUADRATIC RELATIONSHIPS

Many problems involve functions with rules such as:

$$y = 2x^2 + x - 1 \qquad y = 2x(x + 1) \qquad y = (x - 1)^2 + 3$$

All these rules involve an x^2 term, but sometimes this is hidden in the way the rule is written. Such functions are called quadratic functions and the graphs of these functions are parabolas. We are now going to use the graphing utility to plot the graphs of such functions.

Shot-put

Australia's Olympic athlete Jane Flemming competed in the heptathlon. One of her events was the shot-put. It is known that she released the shot about 2 meters above the ground at a speed of about 14 meters per second and at an angle of 45° to the horizontal.

With this information, scientists calculate that the height above the ground, y meters, of Jane's shot is given by the rule:

$$y = 2 + x - \tfrac{1}{20}x^2$$

where x is the horizontal distance the shot has traveled in meters.

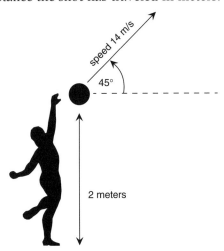

Using your graphing utility, create a blank screen and enter the function given above. You *may* need to use brackets or multiplication signs.

Change the viewing window to obtain a good picture of the graph. A window with these dimensions is suitable.

$$-1 \le x \le 25 \text{ and } -1 \le y \le 10$$

Draw a quick sketch of the graph. Mark the point corresponding to the initial height of the shot.

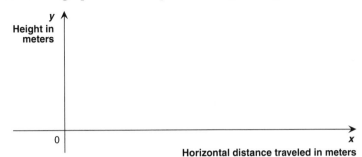

1 The initial height of the shot at the moment that it is about to leave Jane's hand is 2 meters. Verify that the rule calculates this height correctly by substituting $x = 0$.

_____

Use your graphing utility to help you answer question 2.

2 a i How high is the shot after it has traveled 5 meters horizontally from where Jane Flemming released it? _____

    ii Check by substituting $x = 5$ in the rule.

_____

   b i How high is the shot after it has traveled 12 meters horizontally from where Jane Flemming released it? _____

    ii Check by substituting $x = 12$ in the rule.

_____

   c Find the highest point reached by the shot in its flight and mark this point on your sketch. [*Hint:* Ground level corresponds to $y = 0$.] _____

   d Find how far from Jane Flemming the shot will land. Mark this point on your sketch. _____

Kitchen gadget

When items are priced for sale, two factors need to be considered:

● as you increase the price, you receive more money for each item sold (so your profit might increase);

● as you increase the price, you won't sell as many (so your profit might decrease).

Combining these two factors, as the price of an item increases, the profit first increases but then decreases as the price gets too high. So the graph of the profit against the price of an item has the shape of a parabola. So the rule for the profit can be modeled by a quadratic rule.

Suppose that Smith Enterprises invents a new kitchen gadget. Market research suggests that if the gadget is priced at $\$x$, then the weekly profit $P(x)$ in thousands of dollars will be given by:

$$P(x) = -5 + 3x - \frac{1}{4}x^2$$

Use your graphing utility to enter the profit function and draw the graph. You may need to experiment with the viewing window to get a good picture.

1 Draw a quick sketch below and label the axes. Find and mark the point where $x = 0$ and explain what this means for Smith Enterprises.

Use your graphing utility to help you answer question **2**.

2 a i What profit, in dollars, would Smith Enterprises make each week if they charged $5 per gadget? _____

   ii Check by substituting $x = 5$ in the rule. _____

   b What price should Smith Enterprises charge for a gadget to obtain the highest possible weekly profit? _____ What then is the weekly profit? _____ Mark this point on your sketch.

   c What are the break-even points; that is, what price could Smith Enterprises charge to make neither a profit nor a loss? _____ Mark the points on your sketch.

Running a ship

The cost per hour $C(s)$ in thousands of dollars for running a particular ship traveling at a speed of s knots is given by the rule:

$$C(s) = 0.3s^2 - 3s + 12$$

Use your graphing utility to enter the cost function and draw the graph.
You may need to experiment with the viewing window to get a good picture.

1 Draw a quick sketch of the function and label the axes.

Find and mark the point where $s = 0$ and explain what this means.

Use your graphing utility to help you answer question **2**.

2 a i What is the cost in dollars per hour of running the ship
when it is traveling at 3 knots? _____

ii Check by substituting $s = 3$ in the rule.

_____

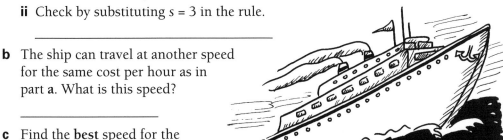

b The ship can travel at another speed
for the same cost per hour as in
part **a**. What is this speed?

_____

c Find the **best** speed for the
ship to run (that is, for
cheapest cost per hour).

_____

What then is the cheapest cost per hour? _____
Mark this point on your sketch.

Holding pen area

A farmer has 15.4 meters of fencing with which to build a rectangular-shaped holding pen for
his sheep. The pen is to be located next to a corner and wall of an existing shed as shown in the
diagram. Fencing is not needed along the shed walls.

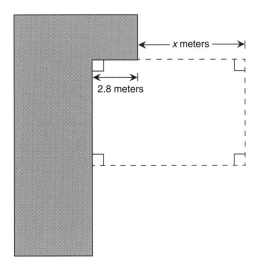

Use the above information to answer the following questions.

1 Show that the dimensions of the pen, in meters, are given by $x + 2.8$ and $12.6 - 2x$.

_____

_____

2 Write a rule, in terms of x, for the area of the pen $A(x)$ in m².

_____

Use your graphing utility to enter the area function and draw the graph. You may need to experiment with the viewing window to get a good picture.

3 a From the graph, find the coordinates of the point that corresponds to the greatest area. _____

   b What is the greatest area? _____

4 What are the dimensions of the length and width of the pen that give greatest area? _____

5 a What is the domain of the area function; that is, what values can x take? _____

   b What is the range of the area function; that is, what values can A take? _____
Can the pen have an area of 50 m²? _____

Sydney Harbor Bridge

The main arch of the Sydney Harbor Bridge is approximately parabolic in shape. It is 503 meters between the two pylons. If x is the number of meters measured horizontally from one of the pylons and $H(x)$ is the height of the arch in meters above water level at the point x, it has been found that:

$$H(x) = \frac{x(503 - x)}{475}$$

where x is the number of meters measured horizontally from one of the pylons and H is the height of the arch in meters above the base of the pylons (water level).

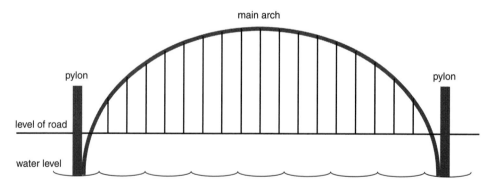

Using your graphing utility, define the arch function and draw the graph. You may need to experiment with the viewing window to get a good picture.

6 a i Find the height of the arch above the water 100 meters from the pylon.
_____

    ii Check using the rule for $H(x)$. _____

  b i Find the height of the arch above the water 300 meters from the pylon. _____

    ii Check using the rule for $H(x)$. _____

  c Where is the arch 100 meters above the water? _____

  d What is the height of the arch at its highest point and how far from the pylon is this?
_____ , _____

The road which runs across the Sydney Harbor Bridge is 52 meters above the water. On the same set of axes, enter and plot a function corresponding to the road at a height of 52 meters.

7 a Find the two points where the arch crosses over the road. _____, _____

   b Work out the length of road between the two points where the arch crosses the road. _____

8 Experiment with different functions in your graphing utility to find the function for the height of the arch of a bridge which is as wide as the Sydney Harbor Bridge but:

   a is only half as high _____

   b is twice as high. _____

The height function for the bridge only applies for a restricted set of values for *x*. To take this restriction into account, the height function could be redefined as:

$$\frac{x(503 - x)}{475} \quad \text{for } 0 \le x \le 503$$

When the height function with this restricted domain is entered into a graphing utility, what you see changes as shown.

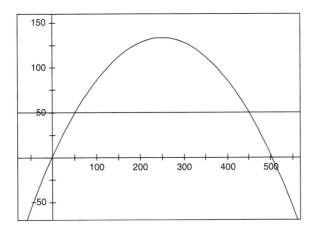

The height function drawn without any restrictions

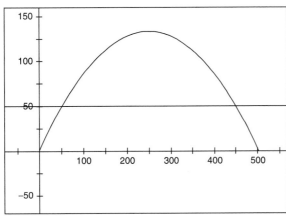

The height function with restricted domain

9 Restrict the height function further so that the graph you get corresponds to the road together with the portion of the arch above the road.
Write down the domain you have used. _____

FITTING QUADRATIC FUNCTIONS TO DATA

Falling object

A stone is dropped from a high bridge into the water.
A camera takes a photograph every 0.4 seconds showing
how far the stone has fallen. The distances are given in
the table for the first two seconds.

Time elapsed (seconds)	0	0.4	0.8	1.2	1.6	2.0
Distance fallen (meters)	0	0.78	3.14	7.04	12.56	19.6

Using your graphing utility, enter and plot the data. We will try to find a parabola which is a
good fit to the data.

1 a Use the rule $y = ax^2$ with different values for a to find a parabola which fits
the data well by eye. Write down the equation
for your quadratic function. _____

  b Use your graph to predict how far the stone
will have fallen after 3 seconds. _____

  c The bridge is 100 meters above the water. About how
long will it take for the stone to hit the water? _____

2 a Find how far the stone fell in the last one-hundredth
of a second before hitting the water. _____

  b Use the information from part **a** to find approximately how
fast the stone was traveling when it hit the water. _____

  c Find how long it took for the stone to fall the
last meter before hitting the water. _____

  d Use the information from part **c** to find approximately
how fast the stone was traveling when it hit the water. _____

  e Compare your answer for part **d** with your answer for part **b**. Which is the more
accurate?

_____

_____

Vehicle stopping distances

Drivers stopping to avoid collisions need to be aware of the factors that affect the distance that the car travels before coming to a complete stop.

Two critical factors affecting the total stopping distance are:

● The *reaction distance*—the distance traveled during the time a driver sees a hazard and the time when he or she applies the brakes.

● The *braking distance*—the distance traveled from the moment the brakes are applied until the car stops.

Both of these distances depend on the speed of the car at the time the driver sees the hazard.

The following data have been obtained for total stopping distance for motor vehicles. The cars used were in excellent mechanical condition and the road and weather conditions were extremely good.

Speed in km/h (s)	10	20	30	40	50	60	70	80	90	100
Total stopping distance in meters (T)	4	7	12	18	25	34	43	54	66	80

Source: *Royal Auto*, October 1990

Using your graphing utility, enter and plot the data.

1 Use the rule $T = as^2$ with different values of a to find a parabola which fits the data well by eye. Write down the rule for your parabola. _____

You may have found it difficult to obtain a good fit in question 1. It is possible to improve the fit by considering the two main factors affecting the total stopping distance. Recall that the total stopping distance is the sum of two distances, the reaction distance and the braking distance. That is:

  total stopping distance (T) = reaction distance (R) + braking distance (B)

Let us look more carefully at the reaction distance. The following data have been obtained for reaction distances for the same speeds as before.

Speed in km/h (s)	10	20	30	40	50	60	70	80	90	100
Reaction distance in meters (R)	2	4	6	8	10	12	14	16	18	20

2 Examine the last table carefully. Find a linear rule of the form $R = ks$ for the data. You should not need to use your graphing utility to do this. _____

Since $T = R + B$, then $B = T - R$. From the two previous tables we can find the table of braking distances.

Speed in km/h (s)	10	20	30	40	50	60	70	80	90	100
Braking distance in meters (B)	2	3								

3 Complete the table above.

Create a blank screen with your graphing utility and plot the data for B against s.

4 Use the rule $B = bs^2$ with different values of b to find a parabola
which fits the data well by eye. _____

5 Using $T = R + B$, write down the rule for the total stopping distance T in terms
of s using your results from question **2** and question **4**. _____

Enter and plot the graph corresponding to this rule on the file or window containing
the original data for total stopping distances.

6 Find the total stopping distance for a fast car traveling at 150 km/h. _____

7 A car took 100 meters to stop from the time its driver saw a hazard.
At what speed was it traveling? _____

8 A car is traveling at 115 km/h when its driver hits the brakes 80 meters before an
intersection. What happens? _____

_____

9 a A police officer investigates an accident scene in a residential street, and observes a
skid mark of about 33.5 meters. At what speed would the officer estimate that the
car was traveling when the brakes were applied?
(If necessary, use the conversion: 10 miles per hour ≈ 16 km/h.) _____

b If you were a lawyer defending the driver of that car, what reasons might you give
in evidence to suggest that the speed estimated in part **a** might be too high?

_____

_____

TRANSFORMATION CREATIONS ON FAMILIES OF QUADRATIC FUNCTIONS

Creations

The creations in this section are based on families of quadratic functions. Use a graphing utility to create the following designs. Record the functions you use. The creations do not need to be exactly the same as the ones shown, but the picture you make should look similar. It will help if you set the viewing window for each before you start.

Most of these creations will work well if you enter the quadratic functions using the form $y = a(x - h)^2 + k$, and experiment with the values of a, h and k. For each creation, two of these values will be fixed and the third will change.

1 Fountain reflections

Adjust the viewing window so that you are looking at the region bounded by:

$$-6 \leq x \leq 6 \text{ and } -30 \leq y \leq 30$$

Sometimes when water is spurting out of a fountain its reflection can be seen. Enter and plot functions to draw a fountain of water such as this and its reflection.

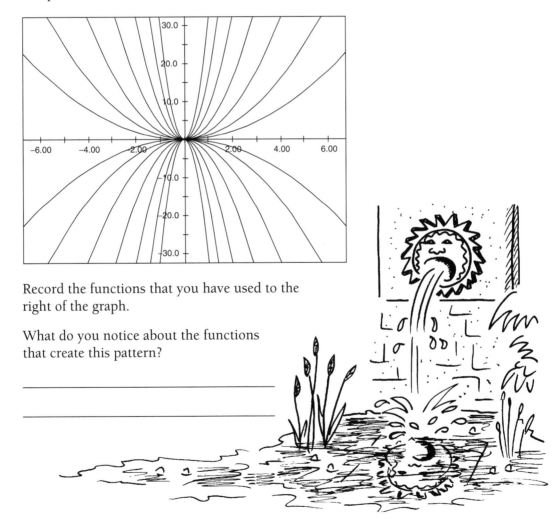

Record the functions that you have used to the right of the graph.

What do you notice about the functions that create this pattern?

_____

_____

2 Fish kite

Adjust the viewing window so that you are looking at the region bounded by:

$$-6 \leq x \leq 6 \text{ and } -20 \leq y \leq 10$$

Japanese fish kites have streamers flying off the central kite. Enter and plot functions to draw a fish kite.

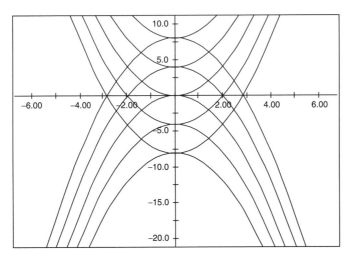

Record the functions that you have used to the right of the graph.

What do you notice about the functions that create this pattern?

3 Curtain

Adjust the viewing window so that you are looking at the region bounded by:

$$-6 \leq x \leq 6 \text{ and } -5 \leq y \leq 25$$

Theatre curtains often drape in a pattern as shown here. Enter and plot functions to draw a similar pattern.

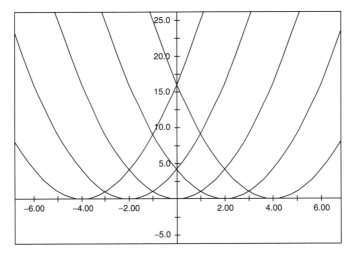

Record the functions that you have used to the right of the graph.

What do you notice about the functions that create this pattern?

4 Parabola diamonds

Adjust the viewing window so that you are looking at the region bounded by:

$$-5 \leq x \leq 30 \text{ and } -2 \leq y \leq 65$$

Diamonds can be found in parabolas! Can you see them? Enter and plot functions to draw a similar pattern.

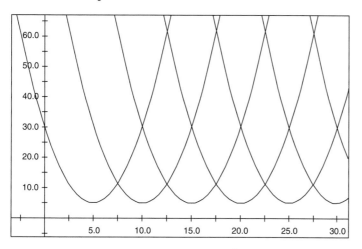

Record the functions that you have used to the right of the graph.

What do you notice about the functions that create this pattern?

5 Running track

Adjust the viewing window so that you are looking at the region bounded by:

$$0 \leq x \leq 20 \text{ and } -5 \leq y \leq 50$$

The lanes on a running track are not all the same length. Outside runners cover a greater distance than inside runners. Enter and plot functions to draw a similar pattern.

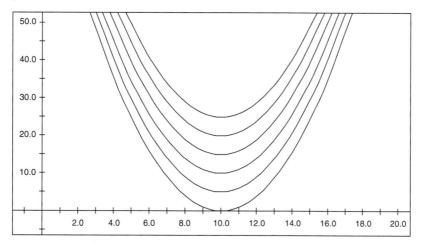

Record the functions that you have used to the right of the graph.

What do you notice about the functions that create this pattern?

6 Necklace

To make the necklace of parabolas, adjust the viewing window so that you are looking at the region bounded by:

$$-15 \leq x \leq 15 \text{ and } -30 \leq y \leq 30$$

All of these parabolas go through the origin so that you will find it easier to enter the functions in the form given by $y = ax(x - c)$. The other points of intersection on the x-axis are equally spaced. The points of intersection on the x-axis do not have to be the same as in the diagram.

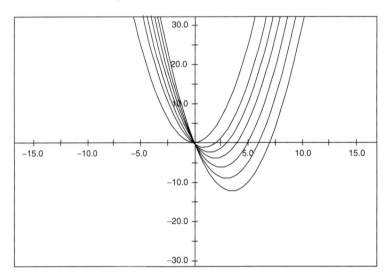

Record the functions that you have used.

_____

_____

7 Create your own

Make up a quadratic creation of your own using quadratic function rules.

On another sheet of paper include a sketch of your creation, a list of the functions you have used, and name the creation.

Quadratic function graphs and constants

After experimenting with the graphs of quadratic functions, you will have noticed how the graphs change when you change the constants. Using your experience with the seven "creations," answer the following questions. You may need to experiment further.

1 What effect does the constant a have on the graph of a quadratic function with rule:

$$y = a(x - 1)^2 + 3?$$

_____

_____

2 What effect does the constant h have on the graph of a quadratic function with rule:
$$y = 2(x - h)^2 + 3?$$

_____

_____

3 What effect does the constant k have on the graph of a quadratic function with rule:
$$y = 2(x - 1)^2 + k?$$

_____

_____

4 What is special about the point given by (h, k) on the graph of a quadratic function with rule:
$$y = a(x - h)^2 + k?$$

_____

_____

5 If a function is defined by the rule $y = a(x - b)(x - c)$, what can be said about the value of the function when either $x = b$ or $x = c$?

_____

_____

3 Scale issues: polynomial functions

THE BIG PICTURE

What are polynomial functions?

So far we have looked at the nature and behavior of linear and quadratic functions. These are examples of functions known as **polynomials**. A function is a polynomial if the terms involve positive integer powers of the independent variable.

Linear functions are polynomials. For example:

$$f(x) = 3x - 1 \quad \text{and} \quad f(x) = 5 \quad \text{are linear functions.}$$

Quadratic functions are polynomials which have an x^2 term. For example:

$$f(x) = 4x^2 - 3x - 7 \quad \text{and} \quad f(x) = (x - 2)(x - 1) \quad \text{are quadratic functions.}$$

There are cubic polynomials with an x^3 term, quartic polynomials with an x^4 term and higher order polynomials. For example, $f(x) = x^7 - 4x$ is a polynomial with an x^7 term. However, the following are not polynomials.

$$f(x) = \frac{1}{x} \qquad f(x) = 2^x \qquad f(x) = 3 \sin (2x + 3) \qquad f(x) = -x^7 + 4x + x^{-1}$$

The big picture

Many function graphs can be deceptive when displayed in a particular viewing window. For example it is possible to miss features such as turning points and intercepts.

The graph of $f(x) = 0.1x^2 - 3x$ looks like a straight line in the viewing window shown on the left in the diagram at the top of the next page, but if you zoom out a few times, it looks like a typical parabola as shown on the right. In the second view, we have the "big picture," because all the essential features are shown.

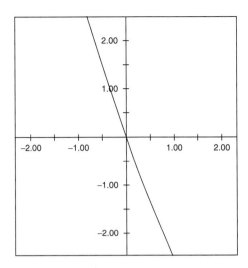
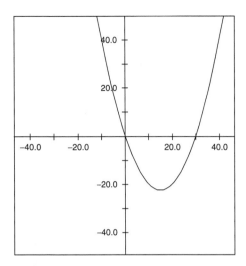

The second view allows us to see that the graph intersects the axis at least twice and has at least one turning point. Further investigation would confirm that this view does reveal the big picture, since outside this viewing window, the graph simply continues to rise on both sides. Once we are confident we have the big picture, we can zoom in to find the coordinates of the turning point and the two intercepts accurately.

For the graph of each function listed below:

- start each one on the default viewing window of your graphing utility;
- zoom as necessary to find the big picture;
- find any turning points;
- find any intercepts with the axes;
- sketch each function on paper, showing all the key features. Label each sketch with the equation.

1 $f(x) = 0.1x^2 - 3x$

2 $f(x) = 120 - x^2$

3 $f(x) = (x^2 - 2)(1 - 0.05x)$

4 $f(x) = 0.1x^3 + 5x$

5 $f(x) = 2x^2 - 0.1x^3$

6 $f(x) = x(1 - x)(x + 10)$

7 $f(x) = x(x^2 - 5)(x - 12)$

8 $f(x) = x^4 - x$

9 $f(x) = x^2(1 - x^2) - 12$

10 $f(x) = x^2(4 - x^2)(x + 13)$

THE RUBBER SHEET

We often have a picture in our mind about how a function looks. For example, we imagine that the graph of a quadratic function will be either an inverted or upright "U" shape. However, the shape of a function graph can appear differently depending on the viewing window.
The scales on the axes are critical. Think of a square section of the X–Y plane as being an extremely elastic "rubber sheet." Changing the scales on the axes is like stretching and shrinking the rubber sheet parallel to the X and Y directions.

1 Enter the function $y = x$ into your graphing utility and then plot it. Change the viewing window to make the graph of the function look:

a steeper

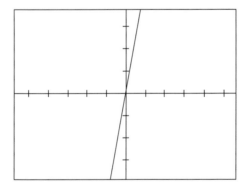

Viewing window:

_____ $\leq x \leq$ _____

_____ $\leq y \leq$ _____

b less steep

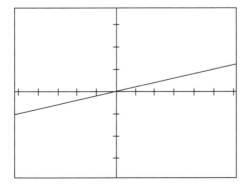

Viewing window:

_____ $\leq x \leq$ _____

_____ $\leq y \leq$ _____

Can you make the graph look like this? _____

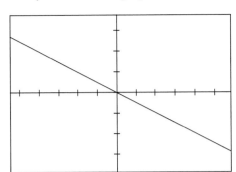

Viewing window:

_____ $\leq x \leq$ _____

_____ $\leq y \leq$ _____

2 Enter the function $y = x^2$ into your graphing utility and then plot it. Make the graph of the function look:

a steeper

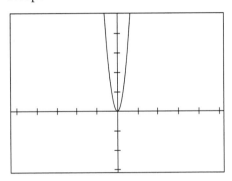

Viewing window:

_____ $\leq x \leq$ _____

_____ $\leq y \leq$ _____

b less steep

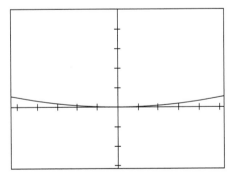

Viewing window:

_____ $\leq x \leq$ _____

_____ $\leq y \leq$ _____

Can you make the graph look like this? _____

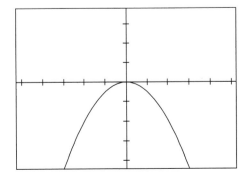

Viewing window:

_____ $\leq x \leq$ _____

_____ $\leq y \leq$ _____

In the following activities, you will be asked to make the graphs of functions appear in more deceptive forms. For example can you make the graph of a quadratic function appear to be a horizontal straight line? First get the big picture. Then select a promising section of the graph and zoom in on it.

3 Draw the graph of the function $f(x) = 0.1x^2 - 3x$. Then change the viewing window to make it look like the following graphs. Record the dimensions of the viewing window.

a

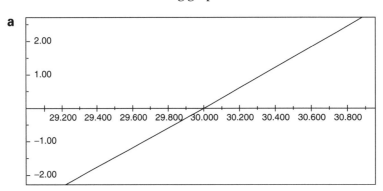

Viewing window:

_____ $\leq x \leq$ _____   _____ $\leq y \leq$ _____

b

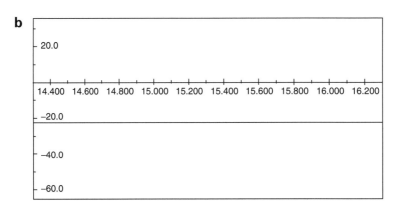

Viewing window:

_____ $\leq x \leq$ _____   _____ $\leq y \leq$ _____

4 Make the graph of the function $f(x) = x^4 - x$ look like the following graphs. Record the dimensions of the viewing window.

a

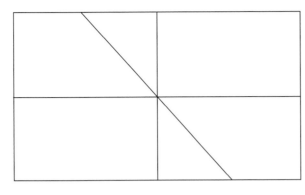

Viewing window:

_____ $\leq x \leq$ _____

_____ $\leq y \leq$ _____

b

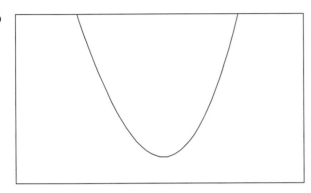

Viewing window:

_____ $\leq x \leq$ _____

_____ $\leq y \leq$ _____

5 Make the graph of the function $f(x) = x^2(1 - x^2) - 12$ look like the following graphs. Record the dimensions of the viewing window.

a

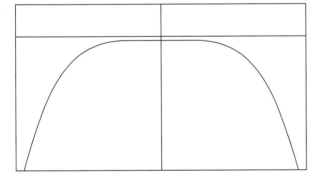

Viewing window:

_____ $\leq x \leq$ _____

_____ $\leq y \leq$ _____

b

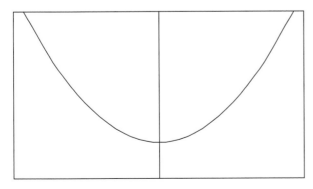

Viewing window:

_____ $\leq x \leq$ _____

_____ $\leq y \leq$ _____

c

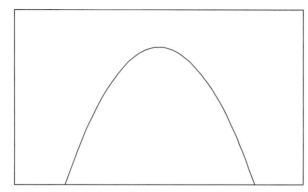

Viewing window:

_____ $\le x \le$ _____

_____ $\le y \le$ _____

d

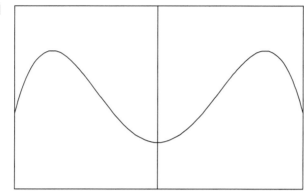

Viewing window:

_____ $\le x \le$ _____

_____ $\le y \le$ _____

6 Make the graph of the function $f(x) = x(x^2 - 5)(x - 12)$ look like the following graphs. Record the dimensions of the viewing window.

a

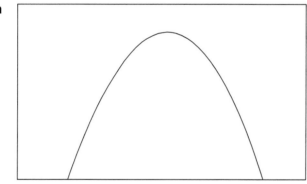

Viewing window:

_____ $\le x \le$ _____

_____ $\le y \le$ _____

b

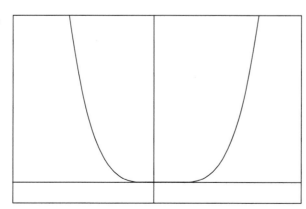

Viewing window:

_____ $\le x \le$ _____

_____ $\le y \le$ _____

c

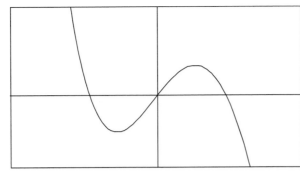

Viewing window:

_____ ≤ x ≤ _____

_____ ≤ y ≤ _____

d

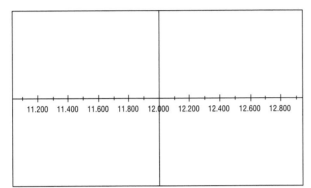

Viewing window:

_____ ≤ x ≤ _____

_____ ≤ y ≤ _____

7 a Make up a function of your own with four quite different views. On another sheet of paper, record the function rule, each view and the dimensions of each viewing window.

b Exchange your rule and your four views with another student and challenge the student to reproduce each view.

Comparing polynomial function families

The following questions ask you to make comparisons between the graphs of some different polynomial function families. They focus on the steepness of each graph in different regions of the X–Y plane. In each question, take time to experiment thoroughly before giving your answer.

1 Is there a vertical line which does not intersect the graph of $y = x^2$? _____

Why? _____

2 Consider the quadratic function $y = x^2$ and the family of functions $y = ax$ where $a > 0$.

a Let $a = 10$. Enter and plot the two functions on your graphing utility. Does the straight line lie "above" the parabola for all positive values of x? If not, why not?

_____

b Choose a larger value of a and repeat part a. _____

_____

c Is it possible to find a value of a so that the straight line lies above the parabola for all positive values of x? Explain your answer. _____

_____

3 Consider the cubic function $y = x^3$ and the family of functions $y = ax^2$ where $a > 0$.

   a Let $a = 0.1$. Enter and plot the two functions on your graphing utility. Does the parabola lie "below" the graph of $y = x^3$ for all positive values of x? If not, why not?

      _____

   b Choose a smaller value of a and repeat part a. _____

      _____

   c Is it possible to find a value of a so that the parabola is always below the graph of $y = x^3$ for all positive values of x? Explain your answer. _____

      _____

4 Consider the quartic function $y = x^4$ and the family of functions $y = ax^3$ where $a > 0$.

   a Let $a = 0.1$. Enter and plot the two functions on your graphing utility. Does the cubic graph lie "below" the graph of $y = x^4$ for all positive values of x? If not, why not? _____

   b Choose a smaller value of a and repeat part a. _____

      _____

   c Is it possible to find a value of a so that the cubic graph is always below the graph of $y = x^4$ for all positive values of x? Explain your answer. _____

      _____

4 Exponential functions: problems and models

EXPLORING EXPONENTIAL RELATIONSHIPS

Paper folding

Take a single sheet of paper.
When you fold it in half, you have two sections of paper. If you fold the sheet in half again, you will have four sections, and so on.
The diagram below illustrates the process.

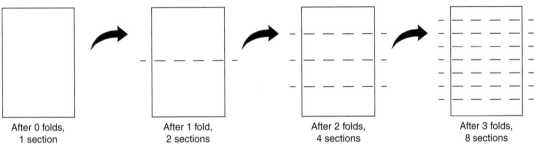

| After 0 folds, | After 1 fold, | After 2 folds, | After 3 folds, |
| 1 section | 2 sections | 4 sections | 8 sections |

1 Complete the table below, which gives the number of sections $S(n)$ as a function of the number of folds n.

Number of folds (n)	0	1	2	3	4	5	6
Number of sections $S(n)$	1	2	4	8			

By observing the table, and thinking about the action of continually folding a sheet of paper in half, we can work out a rule for $S(n)$ in terms of n.

Number of sections after 0 folds $= S(0) = 1$

Number of sections after 1 fold $= S(1) = S(0) \times 2 = 1 \times 2 \qquad = 1 \times 2^1$

Number of sections after 2 folds $= \rule{1cm}{0.4pt} = \rule{1.5cm}{0.4pt} = \rule{2cm}{0.4pt} = \rule{1.5cm}{0.4pt}$

Number of sections after 3 folds $= \rule{1cm}{0.4pt} = \rule{1.5cm}{0.4pt} = \rule{2cm}{0.4pt} = \rule{1.5cm}{0.4pt}$

$$\vdots \qquad \vdots \qquad \vdots \qquad \vdots \qquad \vdots$$

Number of sections after n folds $= \rule{1cm}{0.4pt} = \rule{1.5cm}{0.4pt} = \rule{2cm}{0.4pt} = 1 \times 2^n = 2^n$

The function rule $S(n) = 2^n$ is an example of an exponential function. The independent variable n is the power or exponent and the constant 2 is the base. In general, exponential functions have the independent variable in the exponent.

Note: If we substitute $n = 0$ into the rule $S(n) = 2^n$, the rule gives $S(0) = 2^0$. Since we know that $S(0) = 1$, this means that $2^0 = 1$. In general, if a is not equal to zero we get $a^0 = 1$.

Using your graphing utility, enter and plot the graph of the function $S(n)$. You may need to experiment with the viewing window to get a good picture.

2 a From the graph, how many sections would there be after you had made 10 folds? _____

b Check your answer with your calculator.

3 a From the graph, how many folds will give 8192 sections? _____

b Check your answer with the calculator.

4 Find $S(3.2)$. _____
Explain why substituting 3.2 in the rule for $S(n)$ does not make sense.

_____

Ozone layer

In 1995, the ozone layer was approximately 50 kilometers deep. According to some scientific reports, 1% of the ozone layer is being destroyed each year. This means that in each year the depth is 99% of what it was the previous year.

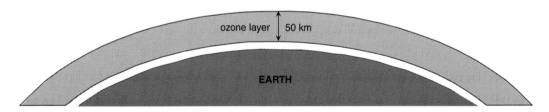

1 Complete the following information relating to the thickness of the ozone layer.

Let t be the number of years that have elapsed since 1995 and $W(t)$ be the width of the ozone layer.

Ozone thickness after 0 years $= W(0) = 50$

Ozone thickness after 1 years $= W(1) = 50 \times 0.99$ $\qquad = 50\,(0.99)^1$ km

Ozone thickness after 2 years $= W(2) =$ _____ $=$ _____ km

Ozone thickness after 3 years $=$ _____ $=$ _____ $=$ _____ km

$\qquad\qquad \vdots \qquad\qquad \vdots \qquad\qquad\qquad \vdots \qquad\qquad\qquad \vdots$

Ozone thickness after t years $= W(t) =$ _____ $=$ _____ km

Note: Again this function is an exponential function with *t* as the exponent and the constant 0.99 is the base. Unlike the example on paper folding, the exponent *t* can take any positive value (not just a whole number value).

Using your graphing utility, enter and plot the graph of the function $W(t)$. You may need to experiment with the viewing window to get a good picture. Use the graph to help you answer the following questions.

2 a Estimate the thickness of the ozone layer at the start of July 1997, when $t = 2\frac{1}{2}$ years? _____

   b Check your answer with your calculator.

3 a During which year will the ozone layer be half of its 1995 thickness? _____

   b During which year will the ozone layer be a quarter of its 1995 thickness? _____

   c During which year will the ozone layer be an eighth of its 1995 thickness? _____

   d Write a simple statement about the time taken for half of the remaining thickness to disappear. _____

_____

_____

4 If the thickness of the ozone layer drops to 100 meters, it will have effectively disappeared. Predict when the ozone layer will have effectively disappeared.

_____

_____

5 Complete the table below.

Number of years since 1995 (*t*)	0	10	20	30
Thickness of ozone layer (*W(t)*) in km	50			

Note: If your graphing utility can create a table of values, you could use this feature here. Use the values in this table to help you answer question 6.

6 a To find the percentage decrease in the thickness of the ozone layer in the first 10-year period, complete the following statement.

$$\% \text{ change } = \frac{\text{new thickness } - \text{ previous thickness}}{\text{previous thickness}} \times 100\%$$

$$= \frac{W(10) - W(0)}{W(0)} \times 100\%$$

$$= \underline{\hspace{2cm}} \%$$

So there is a percentage decrease of _____%.

b To find the percentage decrease in the width of the ozone layer over the second 10-year period, complete the following statement.

$$\% \text{ change} = \frac{\text{new thickness } - \text{previous thickness}}{\text{previous thickness}} \times 100\%$$

$$= \frac{W(20) - W(10)}{W(10)} \times 100\%$$

$$= \underline{\hspace{2cm}}\%$$

So there is a percentage decrease of _____%.

c To find the percentage decrease in the width of the ozone layer in the third 10-year period, complete the following statement.

$$\% \text{ change} = \frac{\text{new thickness } - \text{previous thickness}}{\text{previous thickness}} \times 100\%$$

$$= \frac{W(30) - W(20)}{W(20)} \times 100\%$$

$$= \underline{\hspace{2cm}}\%$$

So there is a percentage decrease of _____%.

d Write a simple statement relating the percentage decrease in the thickness of the ozone layer to the number of 10-year periods that have elapsed.

_____

7 If the ozone layer loses 1% each year, why does it lose less than 10% in 10 years?

_____

_____

Note: The answers to the previous questions illustrate an important property of the nature of exponential relationships. A constant change in the independent variable will create a constant *percentage* change in the dependent variable. This contrasts with what happens for linear functions.

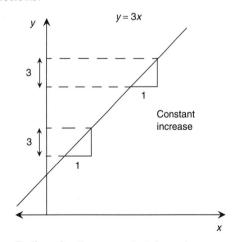

For **linear** functions, a constant change in x produces a constant change in y.

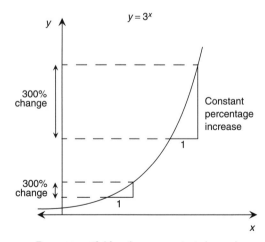

For **exponential** functions, a constant change in x produces a constant percentage change in y.

Movie contract

Stella Rosengren is the hottest movie star of the century. One major studio was so anxious to get her to sign a contract with them, that they offered her a choice of three salary options.

Option A $20 for the first day of work, but overall earnings double for each additional full day of work.

This means that she will make ...$20 for a 1 day contract

$40 for a 2 day contract

$80 for a 3 day contract etc. ...

Option B Two cents for the first day of work, but overall earnings triple for each additional full day of work.

This means that she will make ...$0.02 for a 1 day contract

$0.06 for a 2 day contract

$0.18 for a 3 day contract etc. ...

Option C A flat rate of $100 000 per day for as many full days as the movie is being shot.

This means that she will make ...$100 000 for a 1 day contract

$200 000 for a 2 day contract

$300 000 for a 3 day contract etc. ...

1 Which contract option would you choose? _____

Stella, although a brilliant actor and mathematician in her own right, prefers to leave financial matters to you, her agent. Your job is to give her advice about which offer to accept. First you will need to find how Stella's earnings $E(n)$ in dollars depend on n where n is the number of days that Stella works.

2 a A constant change in n produces a constant percentage change in $E(n)$ for both Options A and B. This means the relationship in either case is:

linear / exponential (*circle the correct term*)

b A constant change in n produces a constant change in $E(n)$ for option C. This means the relationship in either case is:

linear / exponential (*circle the correct term*)

We now build up a formula for the earnings for options *A* and *B* from the information given.

3 a Use the above information to devise a rule for earnings under Option *A*.

$A(n) = $ _____

b Use the above information to devise a rule for earnings under Option *B*.

$B(n) = $ _____

c Use the above information to devise a rule for earnings under Option *C*.

$C(n) = $ _____

4 For what values of *n* are these rules appropriate? Explain your answer.

_____

_____

The film producer has stated that shooting the movie will take between 14 and 21 days.

5 For each of Options *A*, *B* and *C*, use your calculator to find Stella's earnings for a 14-day contract. _____, _____, _____

6 Use the graphing utility to enter and plot the earnings functions for each of the three options. Locate the graphs in the region around 16–20 days.

a Adjust the viewing window to show all three graphs and their points of intersection. Draw a quick sketch of what you see in the viewing window. Label the axes and graphs appropriately.

b Find the coordinates of the points at which the graphs intersect. Add these points to your sketch.

c On another sheet of paper write a report to Stella, outlining your findings and your advice about the best option to take.

Things can go horribly wrong! Owing to a freak storm, shooting the movie is delayed and Stella ends up working for a total of 23 days. In a moment of weakness, the producer agrees to pay Stella under the terms of the original contract. This proves to be quite ridiculously lucrative for Stella!

7 What are Stella's total earnings for 23 days if she takes your advice?

_____

FITTING EXPONENTIAL FUNCTIONS TO DATA

Population change

It has been said that a country's population increases exponentially. The populations of different countries increase at different rates.

This problem looks at whether population data can be said to follow an exponential relationship.

The following table gives the population of Australia (in millions) at the start of each decade from 1900 to 1990.

Year	1900	1910	1920	1930	1940	1950	1960	1970	1980	1990
Number of years (t) elapsed since 1900	0	10	20	30	40	50	60	70	80	90
Population $P(t)$ in millions	3.8	4.5	5.4	6.4	7.3	8.2	10.3	12.7	14.7	17.1

Using your graphing utility, enter and plot the data for $P(t)$ versus t.

The function which we use to fit the data will have a rule of the form:

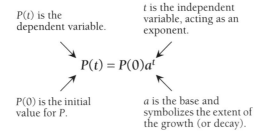

$P(t)$ is the dependent variable.

t is the independent variable, acting as an exponent.

$$P(t) = P(0)a^t$$

$P(0)$ is the initial value for P.

a is the base and symbolizes the extent of the growth (or decay).

1 From the table of Australia's population data (1900–90), read off Australia's "initial" population $P(0)$. _____

The base a is a measure of how quickly the population changes.

2 It has been said that Australia's population increases by about 2% each year. Using this information, give an estimate for a. _____

3 Using your answers for $P(0)$ and a, write the rule of an exponential function that might fit the data.
$$P(t) = P(0)a^t \quad \text{or} \quad P(t) = \underline{\hspace{2cm}} (\underline{\hspace{2cm}})^t$$

Using the graphing utility, enter and plot the function from question **3**. By eye, judge how well your rule fits the data.

4 Try different values for a to find an exponential function which fits the data well by eye. Write down the rule for your exponential function. _____

5 Check your rule for 1990 by comparing the population value obtained for the rule and the value listed in the original table. _____

6 a Use your fitted function to find the population in 1980 and 1981 (that is, $t = 80$ and $t = 81$). Now calculate the percentage annual change (*PAC*) given by the formula:

$$PAC = \frac{P(81) - P(80)}{P(80)} \times 100\% = \underline{\hspace{5cm}}$$

b Repeat part **a** for two successive years of your choice. _____

_____

_____

c How do the answers for parts **a** and **b** compare? _____

_____

d How is *PAC* related to the base *a*? _____

_____

7 In 1993 the actual population of Australia was 17.7 million. How does this compare with the prediction from your fitted function? (Give your answer as a number of persons and as a percentage of the actual population.)

_____

_____

Population doubling times

A population growth rule $P(t) = 3.8\,(1.017)^t$ gives an annual percentage population growth of 1.7% for Australia. A rule like $P(t) = 5.6\,(1.02)^t$ would give an annual percentage growth of 2%.

1 a Write down the annual percentage growth of a country whose population is given by $P(t) = 60\,(1.035)^t$. _____

b A country's population has an annual percentage growth of 4.6%. Its population in 1980 was 54 million. Write down a rule to give the population in millions *t* years from 1980. _____

c If r is the annual percentage growth, and the initial population is $P(0)$, write down the rule which gives the population at time t. _____

A useful way to think about population growth rate is its "doubling time." Doubling time is the number of years for a country's population to double in size.

A rule of thumb for the doubling time d is given by:

$$d = \frac{70}{\text{annual \% change in population}}$$
$$= \frac{70}{r}$$

Thus a country with a current population of one million and a 3.5% annual percentage increase would have a doubling time of $d = \frac{70}{3.5} = 20$ years. That is, 20 years from now the population would be expected to be 2 million.

2 a Use this rule of thumb with $P(t) = 3.8\,(1.017)^t$ to find the doubling time for Australia's population to the nearest year. _____

b How well does your answer for the doubling time seem to work for Australia's actual population values given in the previous table? Do more than one check!

_____

_____

3 For most countries the annual percentage population growth figures are between 1% and 6%. However, their doubling times vary dramatically. Confirm this by completing the following table, using the rule of thumb for doubling time.

Country	Denmark	Finland	Canada	China	Australia	Mozambique	Brunei
Annual growth (%)	0.1		1.1		1.7		6.3
Doubling time (years)		231		44		15	

4 Mozambique's population in 1992 was 16.4 million. Assuming the annual percentage growth figure given in the table above, write down the rule for Mozambique's population in millions at time t (where t represents the number of years elapsed since 1992). _____

Using your graphing utility, enter and plot the function for Mozambique's population at time t.

5 a Find, from the graph, when Mozambique's population will be double its 1992 value. _____

b How does this compare with the doubling time given in the table above?

_____

6 On a separate sheet of paper write a paragraph describing the future population of the world if the exponential models continue to be correct.

Bouncing balls

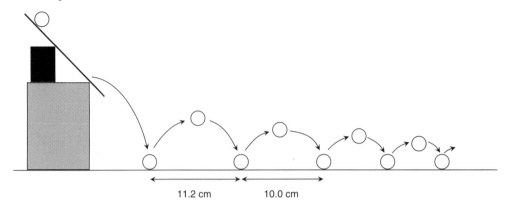

11.2 cm   10.0 cm

A group of students conducted an experiment to test how the horizontal distance that a ball travels between bounces is related to the number of bounces completed. After a number of trials, the students averaged their results and came up with the distances in the following table.

Number of bounces (n)	1	2	3	4	5	6	7	8	9	10	11
Horizontal distance traveled (d cm)	11.2	10.0	9.1	8.3	7.4	6.6	5.8	5.1	4.6	4.4	4.0

Source: *Modelling Real Data Using A Graphic Calculator*, MAV Conference, 1992

Without knowing the relationship between the distance traveled (d) and the number of bounces (n), the students check whether an exponential function may be useful. Recall that successive terms in an exponential function are in a common ratio (for example, double, triple, 30%, 90%).

1 Using your calculator, show that the ratios between successive distances, that is,

$\dfrac{10.0}{11.2}, \dfrac{9.1}{10.0}, \dfrac{8.3}{9.1}, \ldots$, are approximately the same.

This means that the relationship is _____

Using your graphing utility, enter and plot the data in the table using the number of bounces n as the horizontal axis.

2 a Using an exponential function with rule $d = a(b)^n$, find values of a and b so that the exponential graph fits the data well by eye. $a =$ _____, $b =$ _____.

b What is the meaning of b? _____

c According to your fitted rule, after how many bounces will the distance traveled between bounces be about 1 mm? _____

d Using an exponential model implies that the ball will keep bouncing forever. Why does the model imply this? Explain why the ball will not behave this way.

_____

_____

TRANSFORMATION CREATIONS ON FAMILIES OF EXPONENTIAL FUNCTIONS

Creations

The creations in this section are based on families of exponential functions. Use a graphing utility to create the following designs. Make sure to record the functions that you use. The creations do not need to be exactly the same as the ones shown, but the picture you make should look similar. It will help if you set the viewing window for each creation before you start.

You should use the form $y = a(b)^{x-h} + k$ and experiment with the values of a, b, h and k to make these creations.

1 Twisted ribbon

Adjust the viewing window so that you are looking at the region bounded by:

$$-4 \leq x \leq 3 \text{ and } -2 \leq y \leq 3$$

The twisted ribbon design shows interwoven strands, all overlapping at the point $(0, 1)$. Create a design like this.

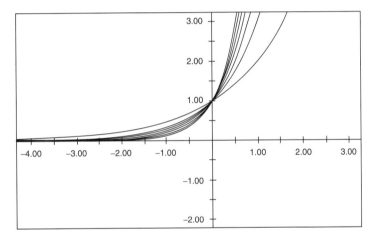

Record the functions you have used to the right of the graph above.

What do you notice about the functions that create this design?

2 Bow

Adjust the viewing window so that you are looking at the region bounded by:

$$-2 \le x \le 2 \text{ and } -0.5 \le y \le 2$$

A bow has been designed, with the knot at the point $(0, 1)$. Create a design like this.

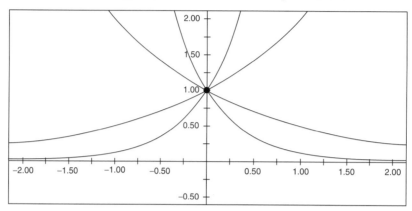

Record the functions you have used to the right of the graph above.

What do you notice about the functions that create this design?

3 Steep slide

Adjust the viewing window so that you are looking at the region bounded by:

$$-7 \le x \le 1 \text{ and } -1 \le y \le 8$$

Playgrounds often have multilane slides, with cushions at the bottom. There is a pattern in the y-intercepts of these functions. Create a design like this.

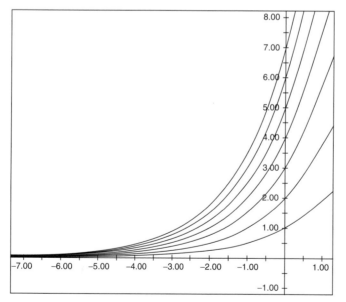

Record the functions you have used to the right of the graph above.

What do you notice about the functions that create this design?

4 Highway bend

Adjust the viewing window so that you are looking at the region bounded by:

$$-3 \leq x \leq 3 \text{ and } -2 \leq y \leq 4$$

The lanes on this highway appear to be getting more narrow as the corner is negotiated, but this is only the effect of perspective. Create a design like this.

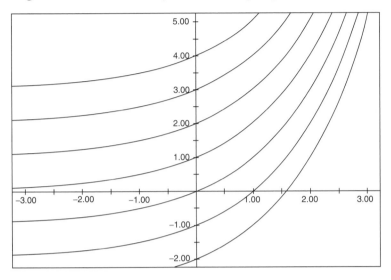

Record the functions you have used to the right of the graph above.

What do you notice about the functions that create this design?

5 Deck chair

Adjust the viewing window so that you are looking at the region bounded by:

$$-6 \leq x \leq 4 \text{ and } -1 \leq y \leq 4$$

This is somewhat similar to the "steep slide" design, except that the lanes appear more parallel, and there is no obvious pattern in the y-intercepts. Create a design like this.

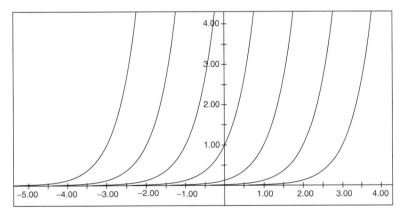

Record the functions you have used to the right of the graph above.

What do you notice about the functions that create this design?

6 Create your own

Make up a creation of your own using exponential function rules. On another sheet of paper include a sketch of your creation, a list of the functions and the name of your creation.

Exponential function graphs and constants

After experimenting with the graphs of exponential functions, you will have noticed that constants such as *a*, *b*, *h* and *k* have a marked effect on the shape of the graph. Using your experience with the six "creations," answer the following questions. You may need to experiment with some more graphs.

1 What effect does the constant *b* have on the graph of an exponential function with rule:

$$f(x) = b^x?$$

_____

_____

2 What effect does the constant *a* have on the graph of an exponential function with rule:

$$f(x) = a(2^x)?$$

_____

_____

3 What effect does the constant *h* have on the graph of an exponential function with rule:

$$f(x) = 2^{x-h}?$$

_____

_____

4 What effect does the constant *k* have on the graph of an exponential function with rule:

$$f(x) = 2^x + k?$$

_____

_____

5 Reciprocal functions: problems and models

EXPLORING RECIPROCAL RELATIONSHIPS

Sharing chocolates

Rory, who missed three months of school, has finally returned to his beloved but small high school. The other students make him feel welcome by giving him a box of his favorite chocolates. The box contains 36 chocolates and he immediately thinks about how he might share them. Each chocolate can be cut into halves or other fractions if required.

1 a Use the information above to complete the table.

	The number n of people who will share the chocolates	The number $C(n)$ of chocolates these people will each receive
If Rory gobbles them all up	1	
If Rory shares them equally with his 2 close friends		
If Rory shares them equally with his 7 good friends		
If Rory shares them equally in his math class of 24	24	
If Rory shares them equally with 72 senior students	72	
If Rory shares them equally with all 144 students at the school	144	

b After choosing a suitable scale and labeling the axes appropriately, plot the points from the above table.

c What was difficult about trying to plot the given points? _____

_____

2 a Explain in words how you calculated the value of $C(n)$ from the value of n, and hence give a rule for $C(n)$ in terms of n. _____

_____

b Check your rule using values from the table in question **1**.

c What sort of values can n take? _____

What sort of values can $C(n)$ take? _____

Using your graphing utility, enter and plot the graph of the function $C(n)$. You may need to experiment with the viewing window to get a good picture.

3 a Assume that it was feasible to cut each chocolate into as many pieces as were required. Use the graph to find what fraction of a chocolate each person would get if Rory shared the chocolates equally between 729 people. _____

b If Rory shared his chocolates with a million people, each would get a tiny amount. Explain how to show this feature with your graphing utility.

_____

_____

4 a There is a point on the graph where the number of chocolates each person shares equals the number of people who are sharing the chocolates. What are the coordinates of this point? (_____, _____)

b Explain how this point can be found by finding the intersection of two graphs.

_____

_____

From question **3**, you will have noticed that as x gets very large, the value of y gets closer to zero. These functions have the property that an increase in one variable leads to a decrease in the other. The graph approaches the x-axis, which is then called the **horizontal asymptote**. If you look at the values of x near zero, you will see that the graph approaches the y-axis, which is then called the **vertical asymptote**.

Functions with rules like $y = \dfrac{36}{x}$, $y = \dfrac{36}{x+7}$, $y = 3 + \dfrac{14}{2x-5}$ have graphs called **hyperbolas**.

All hyperbolas have two asymptotes, and two separate branches separated by the asymptotes.

Functions of this type are examples of **reciprocal functions**. They have the property that an increase in one variable results in a decrease in the other.

Weather balloon take-offs

Picture a weather balloon rising from the ground after take-off. For the purpose of this example, we will assume that the balloon climbs so that its height h meters, at time t minutes $(t \geq 0)$, is modeled by the rule:

$$h(t) = 10{,}000 - \frac{10{,}000}{t+1}$$

Using your graphing utility, enter and plot the graph of the function $h(t)$. Be careful as you may have to use brackets. Adjust the scaling factors and the viewing window so that you can observe the nature of the graph.

1 In which 10-minute period of the first hour of flight is the balloon climbing most rapidly? _____

2 In which 10-minute period of the first hour of flight is the balloon climbing most slowly? _____

3 a Changing the viewing window as necessary, use the graph to find the height of the balloon as accurately as possible, when $t = 180$. _____

  b Use your calculator and the rule for $h(t)$ to calculate the value of $h(180)$.

  _____

4 a Describe what happens to the height of the balloon as time passes.

  _____

  _____

  b Justify your answer to part **a** by explaining what happens to the value of the second term in the formula for $h(t)$ as t becomes large. _____

  _____

  c Find, to the nearest second, when the balloon is 10 meters below its eventual height. _____

Farm fields

Ivan intends to fence off a rectangular field of two hectares ($2 \times 10{,}000$ m^2 = 20,000 m^2) for his prize-winning horses. As the field is to be adjacent to a road, Ivan is not sure how wide to make the side of the field that is to face the road. For instance, if he makes the field too wide, then it will not be deep enough for other possible uses.

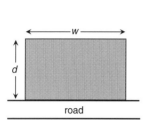
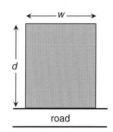
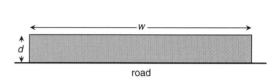

What he would really like is a quick way of calculating how deep the field will be for a given width.

If w represents the width of the field in meters and d the depth of the field in meters, then an expression for the area (A) in square meters will be given by:

$$A = d \times w = 20{,}000$$

He first wishes to establish his options for the field.

1 Write a rule expressing the depth d of the field in meters as a function of the width w meters. _____

Using your graphing utility, enter and plot the depth function that you have written above. The shape of this reciprocal function graph is called a **hyperbola**. It has two branches, one in the first quadrant and the other in the third quadrant.

Since the function is only appropriate for positive values of depth and width, we can restrict it so that only positive values are considered. Restrict the domain to only consider positive values for the width.

2 What depth corresponds to a field width of 200 meters? _____

3 If the depth was to be 50 meters, what would be the width of the field? _____

4 If the depth was to be 63 meters, what would be the width? _____

5 If the field was to be square, what would its dimensions be? _____

According to Ivan, it is not worth considering dimension options that result in either the depth or the width measuring less than 50 meters. For instance, even though a 10 meter $\times$ 2,000 meter field is possible, it is unlikely to be either approved or useful (see the illustration below).

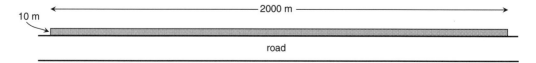

We will now modify the domain of this rule so that the 50-meter restriction is taken into account. Answering the following questions will help you complete this task.

6 a What is the minimum value for the width of the field with the restriction? _____

   b What is the maximum value that the width can take
      without making the depth of the field less than 50 meters? _____

Ivan, although famous for his prized horses, is not very wealthy. Even the cost of fencing his new field will be a severe financial strain. Now that he knows more about the possible dimensions of the field, he wishes to find the dimensions that will minimize the amount of fencing necessary.

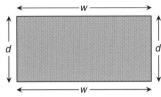

The perimeter of the block, P meters, is given by:

$$P = 2\,(d + w)$$

Since $d = \dfrac{20{,}000}{w}$, it follows that $P(w) = 2\left(\dfrac{20{,}000}{w} + w\right)$

$$= \dfrac{40{,}000}{w} + 2w$$

If we let $f(w) = \dfrac{40{,}000}{w}$ and $g(w) = 2w$ then:

$$P(w) = f(w) + g(w)$$

where $f(w)$ is a **reciprocal** function of w and $g(w)$ is a **linear** function of w.

Using your graphing utility, enter and plot the two component functions $f(w)$ and $g(w)$ over the restricted domain found in question 6. With an appropriate viewing window, you should see a picture like the one below.

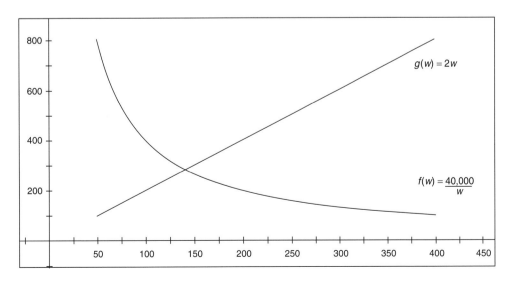

Now, on the same set of axes, enter and plot the perimeter function:

$$P(w) = \frac{40{,}000}{w} + 2w$$

$$= f(w) + g(w)$$

7 Zoom out until you can see the complete picture. Draw a sketch, showing the coordinates of the end points of all three graphs.

Find the values of $f(100)$, $g(100)$ and $P(100)$. What is the relationship between them?

_____

_____

8 a From the graph of $P(w)$, find the value for the width that minimizes the perimeter of the field. _____

  b Find the value of the minimum perimeter. _____

  c Write down the dimensions of the field for minimum perimeter.

  _____ , _____

9 Find the coordinates of the intersection of $f(w)$ and $g(w)$. How do they relate to your answer to question 8? (_____ , _____)

_____

Scuba diving

Scuba divers must not hold their breath as they rise through water or their lungs may burst. This is because the air which they have breathed to fill their lungs underwater will expand as the scuba diver rises and the pressure on the body reduces. At every depth, the diver wants 4 liters of air in her lungs for breathing.

If a diver holds her breath, the volume of the air in her lungs varies with the pressure in the following manner:

$$\text{Volume (at new pressure)} = \frac{\text{original volume} \times \text{original pressure}}{\text{new pressure}}$$

The pressure is 1 atmosphere at the surface and increases by 1 atmosphere for every 10 meters below the surface.

1 A diver takes a 4-liter breath of air at the surface and descends without breathing. Using the formula above, complete the following table.

Depth (*D*) in meters	0	10	20	30	40	50	60
Pressure (*P*) in atmospheres	1	2	3				
Volume (*V*) of air in lungs in liters	4	2					

2 a A diver takes a 4-liter breath of air from her tank at 60 meters. Imagine that she can ascend without breathing. Complete the following table.

Depth (*D*) in meters	0	10	20	30	40	50	60
Pressure (*P*) in atmospheres	1	2					
Volume (*V*) of air in lungs in liters							4

b Find the rule connecting *P* and *D*. _____

Check this rule for *D* = 20, 30 and 40. _____

c Find the rule connecting *V* and *P*. _____

Check this rule for *P* = 3, 4 and 5. _____

d Use algebra to show that $V = \dfrac{280}{D + 10}$.

_____

_____

e Use your graphing utility to draw the graph of the volume of air against depth of the diver in meters. Look at your table and your graph and decide through what depths the diver should be most careful about breathing to avoid bursting her lungs.

_____

_____

TRANSFORMATION CREATIONS ON FAMILIES OF RECIPROCAL FUNCTIONS

Creations

The creations in this section are based on families of reciprocal functions. Use a graphing utility to create the following designs. Make sure to record the functions that you used. The creations do not need to be exactly the same as the ones shown, but the picture you make should look similar. It will help if you set the viewing window for each creation before you start.

You should use the form $y = \dfrac{a}{x-h} + k$ and experiment with the values of a, h and k to make these creations.

1 Hug me

Adjust the viewing window so that you are looking at the region bounded by:

$$-3 \le x \le 5 \text{ and } -3 \le y \le 3$$

Although you will not be able to get a picture of the complete person, it does appear that the graph is about to hug its creator. Create a design like this.

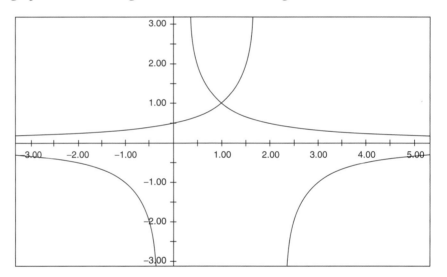

Record the functions you have used.

_____

_____

_____

What do you notice about the functions that create this design?

_____

_____

_____

2 Cross

Adjust the viewing window so that you are looking at the region bounded by:

$$-3 \leq x \leq 3 \text{ and } -3 \leq y \leq 3$$

This creation is a cross formation centered around the origin. Create a design like this.

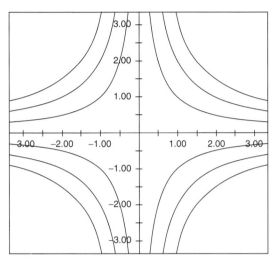

Record the functions you have used to the right of the graph above.

What do you notice about the functions that create this design?

3 Across a cross

Adjust the viewing window so that you are looking at the region bounded by:

$$-3 \leq x \leq 3 \text{ and } -3 \leq y \leq 3$$

Create a design like this. (Note two of the functions are not reciprocal functions.)

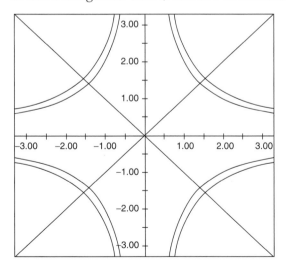

Record the functions you have used to the right of the graph above.

What do you notice about the functions that create this design?

4 Waterfall

Adjust the viewing window so that you are looking at the region bounded by:

$$-3 \leq x \leq 3 \text{ and } -15 \leq y \leq 15$$

The waterfalls in this design all drop around the line $x = 0$. Create a design like this.

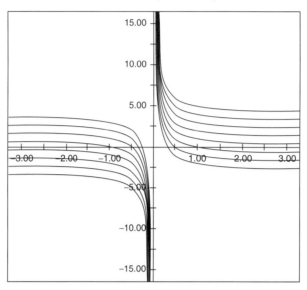

Record the functions you have used to the right of the graph above.

What do you notice about the functions that create this design?

5 Elbows

Adjust the viewing window so that you are looking at the region bounded by:

$$-2 \leq x \leq 4 \text{ and } -3 \leq y \leq 4$$

This design depicts two elbows touching at a point $(1, 1)$. Create a design like this.

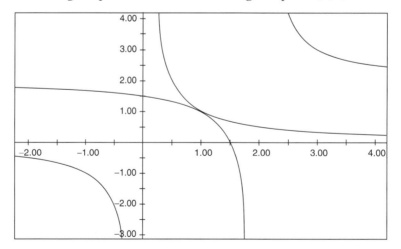

Record the functions you have used to the right of the graph above.

What do you notice about the functions that create this design?

6 Fish kiss

Adjust the viewing window so that you are looking at the region bounded by:

$$-5 \leq x \leq 5 \text{ and } -5 \leq y \leq 5$$

There are two tropical fish here which look to be kissing at the origin. Create a design like this.

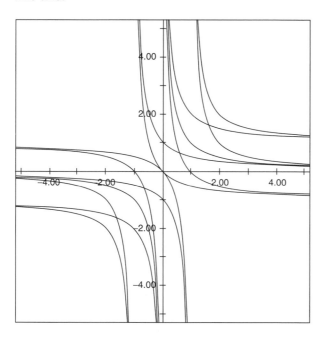

Record the functions you have used.

_____

_____

What do you notice about the functions that create this design?

_____

Reciprocal function graphs and constants

After experimenting with the graphs of reciprocal functions, you will have noticed that constants such as *a*, *h* and *k* have a marked effect on the shape of the graph. Using your experience with the six "creations," answer the following questions. You may need to experiment with some more graphs.

1 What effect does the constant *a* have on the graph of a reciprocal function with rule:

$$f(x) = \frac{a}{x}?$$

_____

_____

2 What effect does the constant *h* have on the graph of a reciprocal function with rule:

$$f(x) = \frac{1}{x-h}?$$

_____

_____

3 What effect does the constant *k* have on the graph of a reciprocal function with rule:

$$f(x) = \frac{1}{x} + k?$$

_____

_____

4 What is special about the point given by (*h*, *k*) on the graph of a reciprocal function with rule:

$$f(x) = \frac{1}{x-h} + k?$$

_____

_____

6 Scale issues: exponential and reciprocal functions

THE BIG PICTURE

When working with exponential and reciprocal graphs, you would have noticed how much adjusting of the scaling and viewing window options was sometimes needed to bring the relevant graph portion into view. Many function graphs can be deceptive when displayed in a particular viewing window.

For instance, the graph of $f(x) = 0.95^x - 1$ looks like a straight line when viewed in the viewing window shown on the left of the diagram, but if you use the viewing window on the right, it looks like a typical exponential graph.

In the second view, we have the "big picture" because all the essential features are shown on the larger graph.

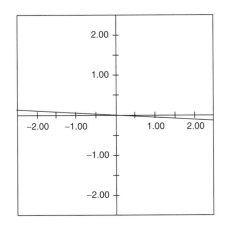 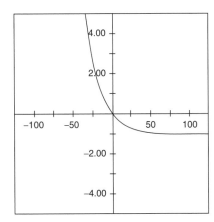

For the graph of each function listed below:

● start each one on the default viewing window of your graphing utility, and then enter and plot the functions;

● zoom as necessary to find the big picture;

● find any intercepts with the axes;

● sketch each function on a sheet of paper, showing *all* the key features.

1 $f(x) = 0.95^x - 1$

2 $f(x) = 0.9^{2-x}$

3 $f(x) = 2^x + 10$

4 $f(x) = 2 - 1.1^x$

5 $f(x) = 25 - 0.2(1.5)^x$

6 $f(x) = 25 - \dfrac{1}{x}$

7 $f(x) = \dfrac{1}{100x - 1}$

8 $f(x) = \dfrac{1}{100 - 3x}$

9 $f(x) = \dfrac{10 - x}{10 + x}$

10 Use your knowledge of the big picture to find all the solutions of the following pairs of equations. Write a convincing argument to explain why there are no more solutions. Put your work on a sheet of paper.

a $y = 2^x$ and $y = -x^2$

b $y = 2^x$ and $y = 2 - x^3$

c $y = 5^x$ and $y = 500 - 5^x$

d $y = \dfrac{1}{x + 1}$ and $y = (x^2 - 9)(1 - x^2)$

THE RUBBER SHEET

We often have a picture in our minds about how a function looks. For example, we imagine that the graph of a quadratic function will be either an inverted or upright "U" shape. However, the shape of a function graph can appear differently depending on the viewing window.

The scales on the axes are critical. Think of a square section of the X–Y plane as being an extremely elastic rubber sheet. Changing the scales on the axes is like stretching and shrinking the rubber sheet parallel to the X and Y directions.

In the following activities, you will be asked to make the graphs of functions appear in more deceptive forms. For example, can you make the graph of an exponential function appear to be a horizontal straight line? First get the big picture. Then select a promising section of the graph and zoom in on it.

1 Draw the graph of the function $f(x) = 0.95^x - 1$. Then change the viewing window to make it look like the following graphs. Record the dimensions of the viewing window.

a

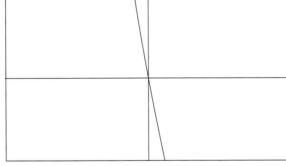

Viewing window:

_____ $\leq x \leq$ _____

_____ $\leq y \leq$ _____

b

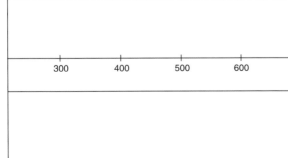

Viewing window:

_____ $\leq x \leq$ _____

_____ $\leq y \leq$ _____

c
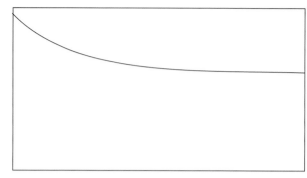

Viewing window:

_____ $\leq x \leq$ _____

_____ $\leq y \leq$ _____

2 Make the graph of the function $f(x) = 2 - 1.1^x$ look like the following graphs. Record the dimensions of the viewing window.

a
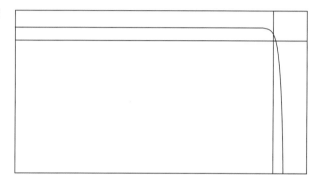

Viewing window:

_____ $\leq x \leq$ _____

_____ $\leq y \leq$ _____

b
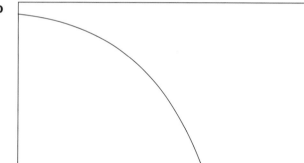

Viewing window:

_____ $\leq x \leq$ _____

_____ $\leq y \leq$ _____

3 Make the graph of the function $f(x) = \dfrac{1}{100x - 1}$ look like the following graphs. Record the dimensions of the viewing window.

a
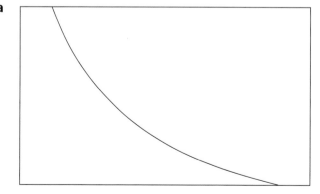

Viewing window:

_____ $\leq x \leq$ _____

_____ $\leq y \leq$ _____

b

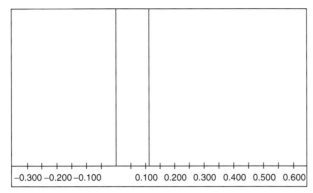

Viewing window:

_____ ≤ x ≤ _____

_____ ≤ y ≤ _____

c

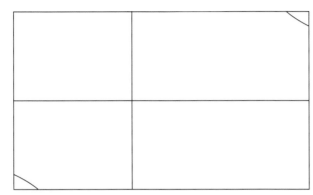

Viewing window:

_____ ≤ x ≤ _____

_____ ≤ y ≤ _____

4 Make the graph of the function $f(x) = 25 - \dfrac{1}{x}$ look like the following graphs.
Record the dimensions of the viewing window.

a

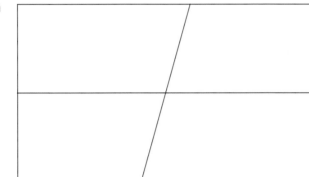

Viewing window:

_____ ≤ x ≤ _____

_____ ≤ y ≤ _____

b

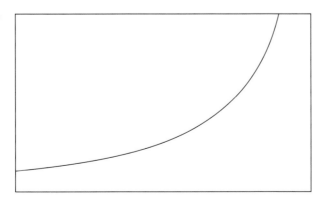

Viewing window:

_____ ≤ x ≤ _____

_____ ≤ y ≤ _____

5 a Make up a function of your own with four quite different views. On a separate sheet of paper, record the function rule, each view and the dimensions of each viewing window.

   b Exchange your rule and your four views with another student and challenge the student to reproduce each view.

6 Can changing the viewing window on the graph of the function $y = 2^x$ make it appear to have:

   a one or more turning points? _____

   b a negative slope somewhere? _____

   c a part that is a straight line? _____

Comparing function families

The following questions ask you to make comparisons between the graphs of some different function families. They focus on the steepness of each graph in different regions of the X–Y plane. In each question, take time to experiment thoroughly before giving your answer.

   a Is it possible to draw a vertical line that never intersects the graph of $y = 2^x$? _____

      If it is possible, give the equation of such a line. _____

      What does this tell you about the asymptotic behavior of exponential functions?

      _____

      _____

   b Is it possible to draw a horizontal line that never intersects the graph of $y = 2^x$? _____

      If it is possible, give the equation of such a line. _____

      What does this tell you about the asymptotic behavior of exponential functions?

      _____

      _____

7 a Can changing the scales and viewing windows on the graph of the function

      $y = \dfrac{1 + x}{1 - x}$ make it appear to have:

      i one or more turning points? _____

      ii a part that is a straight line? _____

   b Is it possible to draw a vertical line that never intersects the graph of $y = \dfrac{1 + x}{1 - x}$? _____

      If it is possible, give the equation of such a line. _____

   c Is it possible to draw a horizontal line that never intersects the graph $y = \dfrac{1 + x}{1 - x}$? _____

      If it is possible, give the equation of such a line. _____

d What does this tell you about the asymptotic behavior of reciprocal functions?

_____

_____

8 Consider the function $y = 2^x$ and the family of functions $y = ax^2$ where $a > 0$.

   a Choose a value of a. Enter and plot the two functions on your graphing utility. Consider whether the exponential function lies "above" the parabola for all positive values of x? Write down when the exponential graph is above the parabola.

_____

   b By experimenting with various values for a, find a value for a so that the exponential graph always lies above the parabola for positive values of x? State your value (or values) of a.

_____

   c Find values of a so that the parabola intersects the exponential graph:

      i once with positive values of x; _____

      ii twice with positive values of x; _____

     iii more than twice with positive values of x. _____

Appendix A
Teacher Notes and Answers

Exploring Linear Relationships

Aims

In this section students will:

- find an algebraic rule for a linear function;
- use the rule and the associated graph to answer questions;
- use a graphing utility to draw a graph;
- enter two or more functions and draw their graphs on the same set of axes;
- change the viewing window in several ways to locate the selected values accurately;
- see that linear functions apply to some everyday situations;
- use a graphing utility to find where straight lines intersect.

Lemonade

Students may not have used function notation previously. Since function notation is used throughout this book, it is important that students have a clear understanding of its meaning. Spend time developing the meaning of x, $P(x)$ and the rule linking x and $P(x)$.

Lemonade with a graphing utility

At the beginning of each of appendices B, C and D there is a "Quick start" section which describes the specific instructions that will achieve steps 1 to 5 for each graphic calculator. If you are using another graphing utility, consult the manual. Work through each of the steps of the "Quick start" page with the students, and check that they have the required graph before proceeding. Information for each step is contained in the appendix. Before entering the function, you may need to show students how to clear functions. Consult the section "How to clear a function rule" in the appropriate appendix.

The answers given in this book can be obtained by careful positioning of the coordinate cursor together with an appropriate level of zooming. At this stage, students are not required to zoom. Student answers are likely to differ slightly from those given and some variation is acceptable. For example, in question **1bi** the answer is given as $2.20 but answers such as $2.23 would be reasonable.

This is the first time students are asked to change the viewing window. Discuss how to zoom out and in. Consult the section "Changing the viewing window" in the appropriate appendix or use your graphing utility manual.

The simplest way to zoom out at this stage for the graphing utilities in the appendices is:
- *CFX-9850G*—from the graph window press **F2** (**Zoom**) and **F4** (OUT).
- *HP 38G*—from the graph window press MENU and ZOOM, select **Out** and press OK.
- *TI-82/83*—press the ZOOM key and select **3 : Zoom out** and press ENTER.

The simplest way to zoom in around the cursor point is:
- *CFX-9850G*—from the graph window press **F2** (**Zoom**) and **F3** (IN).
- *HP 38G*—from the graph window press MENU and ZOOM, select **In** and press OK.
- *TI-82/83*—press the ZOOM key and select **2 : Zoom In** and press ENTER.

Discuss how to record the size of the viewing window. Suggest using $a \leq x \leq b$ and $c \leq y \leq d$. Note that there could be wide variation in student answers.

Lemon and lime

This section asks students to plot two graphs on one set of axes. Consult the section "How to enter and plot more than one function" in the appropriate appendix or use your graphing utility manual.

Mobile phone charges

Note that while it has been sensible to use m as the number of minutes, most graphing utilities require students to enter the function rule using x in place of m. It is important that students become used to interchanging letters in this way and yet interpreting the graphs in terms of the original pronumeral.

Answers

Lemonade (page 1)

1 a $9   **b** $13   **2 a** $6   **b** $10

3 a $2   **b** $2x$ **c** $P(x) = 2x - 3$

4

x	0	1	2	3	4	5
P(x)	−3	−1	1	3	5	7

5 a $9   **b** 3.5 liters; 35 drinks   **c** $11   **d** Angela loses money

Lemonade with a graphing utility (page 2)

Note: Answers read from a graph may not be exact.

1 a 2 liters; $1   **b i** $2.20   **c i** 1.5 liters
   d loses $1   **e i** 2.5 liters   **f** 3.4 liters

2 a $41; dimensions will vary   **b** 5.4 liters   **c** $57

Lemon and lime (page 4)

1 $2.50; 2.5x; 2.5x - 5

2

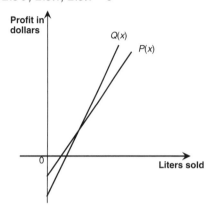

3 a i $1.50 **b i** 2 liters **c i** 3.6 liters   **d i** 3.9 liters

4 a i Angela $0.50   **b i** Kate $1.50   **c i** Angela   **ii** 5 liters

5 a (4, 5)   **b** number of liters sold by both for equal profit
    c profit they would each make if they sold 4 liters

Rohan and Effie (page 5)

1 $T(x) = 3x - 7$

2 a 1.6 liters   **b** $2\frac{1}{3}$ liters   **c i** Rohan; $1.25

  d i Effie; $1.00   **e** Rohan; 0.2 liters or 2 drinks

3 a (6, 11)   **b** number of liters sold by both for equal profit
    c profit they would each make if they sold 6 liters

Mobile phone charges (page 6)

1

Call time	Cost for A(m)	Cost for B(m)	Cost for C(m)	Most expensive	Least expensive
20 minutes	$34.00	$36.00	$43.00	C	A
30 minutes	$46.00	$44.00	$47.00	C	B
40 minutes	$58.00	$52.00	$51.00	A	C
50 minutes	$70.00	$60.00	$55.00	A	C

2 $A(m) = 1.2m + 10; B(m) = 0.8m + 20; C(m) = 0.4m + 35$

3

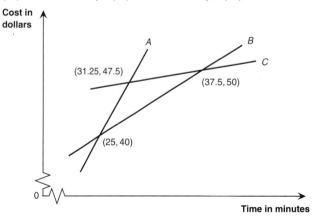

4 From the graph, customers can find out which scheme is best for them by estimating the number of minutes they might use their mobile phone each month and choosing the scheme corresponding to the lowest line segment in their case. So if a customer expects less than 25 minutes of use per month, Scheme *A* is the best. If a customer expects between 25 and 37.5 minutes of use per month, Scheme *B* is best. If a customer expects more than 37.5 minutes of use per month, Scheme *C* is best.

Fitting Linear Functions to Data

Aims

In this section students will:

- learn how to plot data with a graphing utility;
- find rules for functions from a description or a table of data;
- test whether a rule fits data reasonably well;
- interpret calculated values;
- see some situations where linear functions arise;
- create a table of values with a graphing utility.

Arm span versus height

This activity may be used as an individual or group investigation rather than a whole class activity. If done with the whole class, data should be collected well in advance of actual work with the graphing utility.

If this is the first time students are asked to plot data, consult the section "How to plot points" in the appropriate appendix or use your graphing utility manual.

International shoe sizes

You may wish to discuss points such as small sample size; children at different stages of growth; maybe there isn't a strong relationship.

Consider bringing some shoes and/or shoe boxes to class to help motivate discussion.

If your graphing utility cannot create a table of values, you may wish to omit this part. Consult the section "How to create a table of values" in the appropriate appendix or use your graphing utility manual.

Answers

International shoe sizes (page 10)

1 a $S = 0.118(220) - 25 = 0.96$; $S \approx 1$ **b** $S = 0.118(233) - 25 = 2.49$; $S \approx 2.5$

2 Size 8

3 288 mm

4 Values given by its rule should be rounded down to the nearest half size to ensure that the person's foot is not too big.

5 US men's is one size higher.

6 a $S = 0.118L - 24$

7 The two lines are parallel, or have the same slope, with a 1 unit vertical distance between them. This relationship exists because the shoe sizes are always one size different for the same length foot.

8 US women's is 2 sizes higher.

9 US men's shoe size $= S = 0.118L - 24$; US women's shoe size $= 0.118L - 22$

12 A good answer would be $S = 0.15L$; another might be $S = 0.153L - 0.75$ (answers will vary).

13 a An increase of 1 mm in the shoe length increases the continental shoe size by about one-seventh.

   b An increase of about 7 mm in the shoe length increases the continental shoe size by 1.

14 If their rule is $S = 0.15L$, they will get:

   a 36   **b** 37.05   **c** 37.95   **d** 39

These match the continental manufacturers' table very closely.

Transformation Creations on Families of Linear Functions

Aims

In this section students will:

- change the values of a and b in the linear function with rule $y = ax + b$ to see the effect on its graph;
- use functions with restricted domains;
- graph families of linear functions with a graphing utility;
- restrict the domains of functions with a graphing utility.

Creations

Some teachers may like to use "creations" to explore properties of the function families. Others may wish to use them to revise properties. For each creation, the boundaries indicated are only a guide, and students should not waste time attempting to perfect the viewing window dimensions. To set the viewing window for each creation, consult the section "Changing the viewing window" in the appropriate appendix or use your graphing utility manual.

The quickest way to enter the dimensions of the viewing window for the graphing utilities in the appendices is:

- *CFX-9850G*—press SHIFT and **F3** (**V-Window**) and enter the viewing window dimensions.
- *HP 38G*—press the blue key and PLOT and enter the viewing window dimensions.
- *TI-82/83*—press the WINDOW key and enter the viewing window dimensions.

Student designs will differ slightly from those illustrated in the book, while retaining the essential features. The features that should be correct are written in the description. It is not necessary that students attempt every creation.

For creation 7, use color if your graphing utility has it. Students could exchange and see if they can reproduce each other's design. You could also show students how to plot families of functions efficiently. Consult the section "How to plot a family of functions" in the appropriate appendix or use your graphing utility manual.

Transformation creations with restrictions

The set of x values on which a function f is defined is called the *domain*, and the set of y values which the function takes is its *range*. Unfortunately, many graphing utilities use the term "range" loosely, including using it instead of domain. We have tried to be precise. If this is the first time students are asked to graph a function with a restricted domain, consult the section "How to restrict the domain of a function" in the appropriate appendix or use your graphing utility manual.

Answers

Creations (page 15)

1 *Rain:* $y = x + 3$, $y = x + 2$, $y = x + 1$, $y = x$, $y = x - 1$, $y = x - 2$, $y = x - 3$

2 *Horizon:* $y = 4$, $y = 2$, $y = 1$, $y = 0.5$, $y = 0.75$, $y = 0.125$, $y = 0.062$

3 *Triangle:* $y = 3x + 10$, $y = -3x + 10$, $y = -5$

4 *Diamonds:* $y = x$, $y = x + 2$, $y = x - 2$, $y = -x$, $y = -x + 2$, $y = -x - 2$

5 *Windmill:* $y = 5x$, $y = -5x$, $y = 0.2x$, $y = -0.2x$

6 *Sparkler:* $y = x$; $y = \frac{3}{5}x + 2$, $y = 5$, $y = -x + 7$, $y = -x + 10$, $y = 3x - 10$, $y = -3x + 20$

Linear function graphs and constants (page 18)

1 a The line slopes up from left to right.
  b The line slopes down from left to right.
  c The line slopes steeply up from left to right, close to vertical.
  d The line is close to horizontal, and slopes up gently from left to right.

2 a Cuts y-axis above x-axis.
  b Cuts y-axis below x-axis.
  c Cuts y-axis near origin.

3 The values of a are the same.

Transformation creations with restrictions (page 19)

1 *Mountains:* $y = x - 2 (x \leq 0)$, $y = x (x \leq 0)$, $y = x + 2 (x \leq 0)$, $y = x + 4 (x \leq 0)$,
  $y = -x - 2 (x \geq 0)$, $y = -x (x \geq 0)$, $y = -x + 2 (x \geq 0)$, $y = -x + 4 (x \geq 0)$

2 *Peaks:* $y = x + 2 (x \leq 0)$, $y = 2x + 4 (x \leq 0)$, $y = 3x + 6 (x \leq 0)$, $y = 4x + 8 (x \leq 0)$,
  $y = -x + 2 (x \geq 0)$, $y = -2x + 4 (x \geq 0)$, $y = -3x + 6 (x \geq 0)$, $y = -4x + 8 (x \geq 0)$

3 *Triangle:* $y = -5 (-5 \leq x \leq 5)$, $y = 3x + 10 (-5 \leq x \leq 0)$, $y = -3x + 10 (0 \leq x \leq 5)$

4 *Star:* $y = -5 (-5 \leq x \leq 5)$, $y = 3x + 10 (-5 \leq x \leq 0)$, $y = -3x + 10 (0 \leq x \leq 5)$ and
  $y = 8 (-5 \leq x \leq 5)$, $y = -3x - 7 (-5 \leq x \leq 0)$, $y = 3x - 7 (0 \leq x \leq 5)$

Exploring quadratic relationships

Aims

In this section students will:

- work with quadratic functions and their graphs;
- use brackets and order of operations to enter functions into a graphing utility;
- see some situations where quadratic functions arise;
- find, using a graph, the greatest or least values of a function;
- restrict the domain of a function with a graphing utility.

Shot-put

You might like to discuss how an equation like $y = 2 + x - \frac{1}{20}x^2$ arises in a situation like this (for example, the effect of gravity, no air resistance).

Explain how to enter a term like x^2. Also, you may need to discuss what constitutes a "good picture." In this case, it should include the turning point and intercepts with the axes.

Sydney Harbor Bridge

The set of x values on which a function f is defined is called the *domain*, and the set of y values which the function takes is its *range*. Unfortunately, many graphing utilities use the term "range" loosely, including using it instead of domain. We have tried to be precise. If this is the first time students are asked to graph a function with a restricted domain, consult the section "How to restrict the domain of a function" in the appropriate appendix or use your graphing utility manual.

Answers

Shot-put (page 22)

Sketch should look like this:

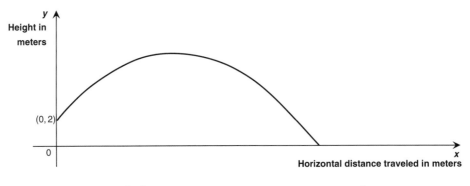

2 a i 5.75 meters   **b i** 6.8 meters   **c** 7 meters   **d** 21.8 meters

Kitchen gadget (page 23)

1 $P(0) = -5$. If the gadgets are given away for free, Smith Enterprises loses $5,000 per week.

2 a i $3,750   **b** $6; $4,000   **c** $2; $10

Running a ship (page 24)

1 $C(0) = 12$; it costs $12,000 to run the ship while standing still.

2 a i $5,700   **b** 7 knots   **c** 5 knots

Holding pen area (page 25)

1 The length of the pen is $(x + 2.8)$ meters (from the diagram). If w meters is the width, then $x + w + (x + 2.8) = 15.4$ (amount of fencing available is 15.4 meters), so $w = 15.4 - x - (x + 2.8) = 12.6 - 2x$.

2 $A(x) = (x + 2.8)(12.6 - 2x)$

3 a $(1.75, 41.4)$ **b** 41.4 sq. meters

4 a 4.55 meters by 9.1 meters

5 a $0 \leq x \leq 6.3$ **b** $0 \leq A(x) \leq 41.4$; no

Sydney Harbor Bridge (page 26)

1 a i 84.84 meters   **b i** 128.2 meters
  c 126 meters and 377 meters from the pylon
  d 133.2 meters; 251.5 meters

2 a $(55.15, 52)$; $(447.85, 52)$ **b** 392.7 meters

3 a $H(x) = \dfrac{x(503 - x)}{950}$ **b** $H(x) = \dfrac{2x(503 - x)}{475}$

4 $55.15 \leq x \leq 447.85$

Fitting Quadratic Functions to Data

Aims

In this section students will:

- fit a quadratic function by eye to given data values;
- use a fitted quadratic function to predict values not present in the given data;
- see some situations where quadratic functions arise.

Falling object

If this is the first time students are asked to plot data, consult the section "How to plot points" in the appropriate appendix or use your graphing utility manual.

Students may experience some difficulty calculating the rates of change in this question, particularly in question **2d**. Discuss how to do this.

Vehicle stopping distances

You might like to discuss how braking distance varies as the square of the speed (this involves kinetic energy). Make sure that students don't clear the data from the table (they could simply turn off plots or use a new file to avoid this). Also, note that in questions **7** and **8**, only the braking distance is involved.

Answers

Falling object (page 28)

1 a $y = 4.9x^2$ **b** 44.1 meters   **c** 4.518 seconds

2 a 0.44 meters   **b** 44 meters/second   **c** 0.023 seconds

   d 43 meters/second

   e The last one-hundredth of a second is more accurate, because the stone has more nearly reached its final speed.

Vehicle stopping distances (page 29)

1 $T = 0.009s^2$

2 $R = 0.2s$

3

Speed in km/h (s)	10	20	30	40	50	60	70	80	90	100
Braking distance in meters (B)	2	3	6	10	15	22	29	38	48	60

4 $B = 0.006s^2$

5 $T = 0.2s + 0.006s^2$

6 ~165 meters, assuming a good car and dry roads

7 ~113 km/h

8 The car stops just before it enters the intersection ($B = 79.4$).

9 a about 75 km/h

   b Road conditions and mechanical condition of car not optimal.

Transformation Creations on Families of Quadratic Functions

Aims

In this section students will:

- change constants in a quadratic function rule to see the effect on the shape and position of its graph;
- graph families of quadratic functions with a graphing utility;
- see that the two forms $y = a(x - h)^2 + k$ and $y = a(x - b)(x - c)$ give different information about the graph.

Creations

Some teachers may like to use "creations" to explore properties of the function families. Others may wish to use them to revise properties. For each creation, the boundaries indicated are only a guide, and students should not waste time attempting to perfect the viewing window dimensions. To set the viewing window for each creation, consult the section "Changing the viewing window" in the appropriate appendix or use your graphing utility manual.

The quickest way to enter the dimensions of the viewing window for the graphing utilities in the appendices is:

● *CFX-9850G*—press SHIFT and **F3** (**V-Window**) and enter the viewing window dimensions.
● *HP 38G*—press the blue key and PLOT and enter the viewing window dimensions.
● *TI-82/83*—press the WINDOW key and enter the viewing window dimensions.

Student designs will differ slightly from those illustrated in the book, while retaining the essential features. The features that should be correct are written in the description. It is not necessary that students attempt every creation.

You will need to show students how to plot families of functions. Consult the section "How to plot a family of functions" in the appropriate appendix or use your graphing utility manual.

Answers

Creations (page 31)

1 *Fountain reflections:* $y = \pm 0.5x^2, \pm x^2, \pm 2x^2, \pm 4x^2, \pm 16x^2, \pm 40x^2$

2 *Fish kite:* $y = \pm x^2 + 4, y = \pm x^2 - 4, y = \pm x^2 + 8, y = \pm x^2 - 8$

3 *Curtain:* $y = x^2, y = (x + 4)^2, y = (x \pm 2)^2$

4 *Parabola diamonds:* $y = (x - 5)^2 + 5, y = (x - 10)^2 + 5, y = (x - 15)^2 + 5, y = (x - 20)^2 + 5, y = (x - 25)^2 + 5, y = (x - 30)^2 + 5$

5 *Running track:* $y = (x - 10)^2, y = (x - 10)^2 + 5, y = (x - 10)^2 + 5, y = (x - 10)^2 + 10, y = (x - 10)^2 + 15, y = (x - 10)^2 + 20, y = (x - 10)^2 + 25$

6 *Necklace:* $y = x^2, y = x(x - 2), y = x(x - 4), y = x(x - 5), y = x(x - 6), y = x(x - 7)$

Quadratic function graphs and constants (page 34)

1 If $a > 0$, the parabola is concave up; if $a < 0$, the parabola is concave down; if $|a|$ is large, the parabola is narrow about the line $x = 1$; if $|a|$ is small, the parabola is wide about the line $x = 1$.

2 Moves graph h units from the y-axis in a horizontal direction (if $h > 0$, moves to the right; if $h < 0$, moves to the left).

3 Moves graph k units in a vertical direction (if $k > 0$, moves up; if $k < 0$, moves down).

4 It is a turning point or vertex, and corresponds to the maximum or minimum of the quadratic function.

5 It equals 0. The graph crosses the x-axis at these points.

The Big Picture

Aims

In this section students will:

● use zooming to help to get a big picture of the graph of a function;
● see the shape of graphs of polynomial functions other than linear and quadratic;
● see that some polynomial functions change very rapidly;
● use the big picture to help determine the number of turning points and intercepts of a polynomial graph.

Answers

The big picture (page 36)

The answers for questions 1 to 10 show the turning point, intercepts and the graphs.

1 Turning point $(15, -22.5)$;
intercepts $(0, 0)$ and $(30, 0)$

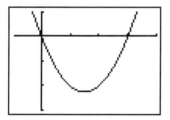

2 Turning point $(0, 120)$;
intercepts $(\pm 10.95, 0)$ and $(0, 120)$

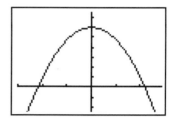

3 Turning point $(-0.05, \ 2.002), (13.4, 58.6)$; intercepts $(\pm 1.41, 0), (20, 0)$ and $(0, -2)$

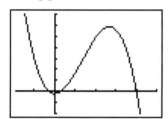

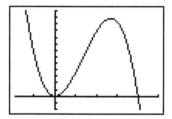

4 Turning point, none;
intercept $(0, 0)$

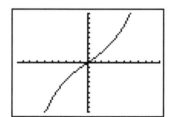

5 Turning points $(0, 0)$ and $(13.3, 118.5)$;
intercepts $(0, 0)$ and $(20, 0)$

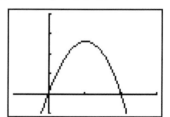

6 Turning points $(0.512, 2.626)$ and $(-6.51, -170.6)$; intercepts $(0, 0)$, $(1, 0)$ and $(-10, 0)$

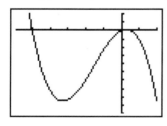

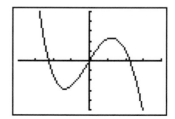

7 Turning points $(1.24, 46.2)$, $(-1.33, -57.3)$ and $(9.09, -2,053)$; intercepts $(\pm 2.236, 0)$, $(0, 0)$
and $(12, 0)$

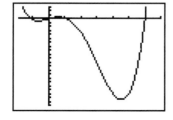

8 Turning point $(0.63, -0.472)$;
   intercepts $(0, 0)$ and $(1, 0)$

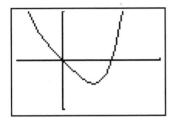

9 Turning points $(0, -12)$, $(\pm 0.707, -11.75)$;
   intercept $(0, -12)$

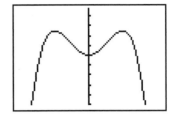

10 Turning points $(0, 0)$, $(-1.39, 46.39)$, $(1.43, 57.69)$ and $(-10.44, -29.296)$;
   intercepts $(0, 0)$ and $(\pm 2, 0)$ and $(-13, 0)$

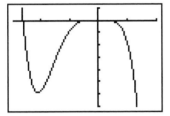   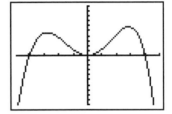

The Rubber Sheet

Aims

In this section students will:

- see how the graph of a function can look very different in different viewing windows;
- learn how to give a deceptive picture of a function;
- find that not all features of a graph can be changed by changing the viewing window.

The various options for zooming in on a section are explained in "Using scaling/zooming options" in the appropriate appendix. For the CFX-9850G the Box option from the Zoom menu is useful here. For the HP 38G use the Box option accessed via Zoom in the graph window Menu. For the TI-82/83 use Zoom and ZBox. For other graphing utilities, consult your manual.

Comparing polynomial function families

Question **2** is designed to show students that a quadratic eventually has larger values than any linear function. Question **3** is designed to show students that no matter how flat the parabola, it is still above the cubic graph for some positive values of x. Similar ideas are brought out in question **4**. For question **2**, students will need to zoom out to get the "big picture." For questions **3** and **4**, they will need to zoom in near the origin.

Answers

The Rubber Sheet (page 38)

4 a *Hint*: a small viewing window around the point $(0, 0)$.
   b *Hint*: a small viewing window around the point $(0.64, -0.46)$.

5 a *Hint:* make the range of *y*-values very large.
   b *Hint:* a small viewing window around the point $(0, -12)$.
   c *Hint:* a small viewing window around the point $(-0.7, -11.7)$.
   d *Hint:* a small viewing window around the point $(0, -12)$ and then stretch the *y*-axis.

6 a *Hint:* a small viewing window around the point $(1.24, 46.18)$.
   b *Hint:* a large viewing window around the point $(0, 5)$, increasing the range of *y*-values.
   c *Hint:* a large viewing window around the origin, increasing the range of *y*-values.
   d *Hint:* a small viewing window around the point $(0, 12)$.

Comparing polynomial function families (page 43)

1 No, eventually the parabola crosses any vertical straight line.
2 a No; they cross at $x = 10$.
   c No; they cross at $x = a$. The parabola is then above the straight line for $x > a$.
3 a No; they cross at $x = 0.1$.
   c No; they cross at $x = a$. The parabola lies above the cubic graph for $0 < x < a$.
4 a No; they cross at $x = 0.1$.
   c No; they cross at $x = a$. The cubic graph lies above the graph of $y = x^4$ for $0 < x < a$.

Exploring Exponential Relationships

Aims

In this section students will:
- work with exponential functions and their graphs;
- learn about some important characteristics of exponential functions;
- see some situations where exponential functions arise.

Paper folding

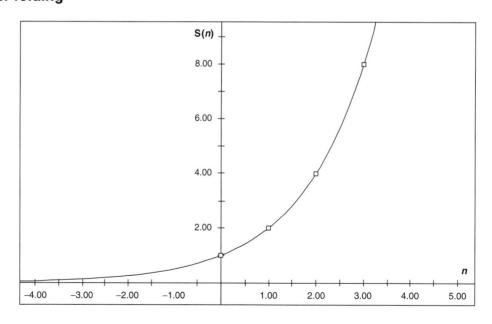

Note: Although the function has been plotted as though the number of folds, *n* can take any value, in fact only whole number values are possible for *n* in this case. In the graph above, the first four possible points have been marked. When interpreting this graph, keep in mind that only whole number values for *n* are possible.

Movie contract

Some graphing utilities will use scientific notation to describe coordinates. You may need to discuss the meaning of this notation.

In general, we can use the fitted function to work out the percentage annual change from *any* year (*t*) to the following year (*t* + 1) as follows.

Suppose the rule is $P(t) = 3.8 (1.017)^t$

$$\text{Percentage annual change} = \frac{\text{population in year } (t+1) - \text{population in year } t}{\text{population in year } t} \times 100\%$$

$$= \frac{3.8(1.017)^{t+1} - 3.8(1.017)^t}{3.8(1.017)^t} \times 100\%$$

$$= \frac{(1.017)^{t+1} - (1.017)^t}{(1.017)^t} \times 100\%$$

$$= (1.017 - 1) \times 100\%$$

$$= 1.7\%$$

Answers

Paper folding (page 45)

1 See table below.

Number of folds (*n*)	0	1	2	3	4	5	6
Number of sections (*S*)	1	2	4	8	16	32	64

2 a 1024 sections

3 a 13 folds

4 9.19; 3.2 is not a whole number

Ozone layer (page 46)

1 50×0.99^2; 50×0.99^3; 50×0.99^6

2 49 km

3 a in the year 2064   **b** in the year 2133
  c in the year 2202   **d** Reduces to half previous value every 69 years.

4 618 years from 1995, or 2613

5 See table below.

Number of years since 1995 (*t*)	0	10	20	30
Thickness of ozone layer in km (*W(t)*)	50	45.2	40.9	37.0

6 a −9.56%; 9.56%   **b** −9.56%; 9.56%   **c** −9.56%; 9.56%
  d Every 10 years the ozone layer reduces by 9.56%.

7 After each year it loses 1% of a smaller thickness than the original 50 km. So after 10 years it loses less than 10% of its original thickness.

Movie contract (page 49)

2 a exponential   **b** linear

3 a $A(n) = 20 \times 2^{n-1}$ **b** $B(n) = 0.02 \times 3^{n-1}$ **c** $C(n) = 100,000n$

4 Works for positive integers.

5 Option A: $163,840; Option B: $31,886.46; Option C: $1,400,000

6 b $A(n)$ and $B(n)$ intersect at $(17.41, 1,741,000)$
$A(n)$ and $C(n)$ intersect at $(17.65, 1,765,000)$
$B(n)$ and $C(n)$ intersect at $(18.03, 2,689,000)$

  c Since Stella only works for full days, she only needs to consider which graph is highest at integer values. From the graph and the intersection points, her best options are: if she expects to work no more than 17 days, then option C is best; if she expects to work exactly 18 days, then option A is best; if she expects to work for at least 19 days, then option B is best.

7 Option A: $83,886,080; Option B: $627,621,192; Option C: $2,300,000

Fitting Exponential Functions to Data

Aims

In this section students will:

● learn about the halving and doubling times for exponential functions;

● calculate percentage annual change for population growth;

● fit exponential functions to a data set by eye;

● see some situations where exponential functions arise.

Population change

If this is the first time students are asked to plot data, consult the section "How to plot points" in the appropriate appendix or use your graphing utility manual.

Bouncing balls

You may wish to have students actually do this experiment and collect their own data, using wet tennis balls on a surface that the water will mark.

Answers

Population change (page 51)

1 3.8 (millions)   **2** 1.02

3 $P(t) = 3.8(1.02)^t$ **4** $P(t) = 3.8(1.017)^t$ (small variations likely)

5 by rule: 17.3; by table: 17.1

6 c Their values are the same.   **d** $PAC = a - 1$

7 300,000; 1.69% approximately; answers will vary

Population doubling times (page 52)

1 a 3.5%   **b** $P(t) = 54(1.046)^t$ **c** $P(t) = P(0)\left(1 + \dfrac{r}{100}\right)^t$

2 a 41 years   **b** Estimate is pretty close.

3

Country	Denmark	Finland	Canada	China	Australia	Mozambique	Brunei
Annual growth (%)	0.1	0.3	1.1	1.6	1.7	4.7	6.3
Doubling time (yrs)	700	231	64	44	41	15	11

4 $P(t) = 16.4(1.047)^t$

5 a 15 years   **b** agrees

Bouncing balls (page 54)

1 Exponential

2 a $d = 12.5(0.9)^n$

b ratio of successive terms of a "decay" function

c 46 bounces

d From the model, no matter what the value of n, $d > 0$ so this implies that the ball keeps moving to the right. However, we know from experience that the ball will eventually start rolling and then come to a stop. It stops bouncing because it does not have perfect elasticity; it eventually stops rolling because of friction.

Transformation Creations on Families of Exponential Functions

Aims

In this section students will:

- see how changing constants in an exponential function rule affects the shape and position of the graph;
- learn how to translate the graphs of exponential functions to the left and right;
- learn how to translate the graphs of exponential functions up and down.

Creations

Some teachers may like to use "creations" to explore properties of the function families. Others may wish to use them to revise properties. For each creation, the boundaries indicated are only a guide, and students should not waste time attempting to perfect the viewing window dimensions. To set the viewing window for each creation, consult the section "Changing the viewing window" in the appropriate appendix or use your graphing utility manual.

The quickest way to enter the dimension of the viewing window for the graphing utilities in the appendices is:

- *CFX-9850G*—press SHIFT and **F3** (**V-Window**) and enter the viewing window dimensions.
- *HP 38G*—press the blue key and PLOT and enter the viewing window dimensions.
- *TI-82/83*—press the WINDOW key and enter the viewing window dimensions.

Student designs will differ slightly from those illustrated in the book, while retaining the essential features. The features that should be correct are written in the description. It is not necessary that students attempt every creation.

You will need to show students how to plot families of functions. Consult the section "How to plot a family of functions" in the appropriate appendix or use your graphing utility manual.

Answers

Creations (page 55)

1 *Twisted ribbon:* $y = 2^x$, $y = 3^x$, $y = 5^x$, $y = 6^x$, $y = 7^x$, $y = 8^x$

2 *Bow:* $y = 2^x$, $y = 0.5^x$, $y = 8^x$, $y = 0.125^x$

3 *Steep slide:* $y = 2^x$, $y = 2 \times 2^x$, $y = 3 \times 2^x$, $y = 4 \times 2^x$, $y = 5 \times 2^x$, $y = 6 \times 2^x$, $y = 7 \times 2^x$

4 *Highway bend:* $y = 2^x$, $y = 2^x \pm 1$, $y = 2^x \pm 2$, $y = 2^x \pm 3$

5 *Deck chair:* $y = 10^{x-3}$, 10^{x-2}, 10^{x-1}, 10^x, 10^{x+1}, 10^{x+2}, 10^{x+3}

Exponential function graphs and constants (page 58)

1 If $0 < b < 1$, graph falls from left to right; if $b > 1$, graph rises from left to right. The graph rises more quickly for larger values of b.

2 Changes y-intercept to $(0, a)$ and stretches the graph vertically.

3 Moves the graph left ($h < 0$) or right ($h > 0$) by h units.

4 Moves the graph up ($k > 0$) or down ($k < 0$) by k units.

Exploring Reciprocal Relationships

Aims

In this section students will:

● work with reciprocal functions and their graphs;

● see some situations involving reciprocal functions and hyperbola graphs;

● learn about asymptotes and their interpretation;

● encounter the difficulties of plotting functions which are changing very rapidly.

Sharing the chocolates

Near a vertical asymptote, functions change very rapidly, and so care must be taken when interpreting function values from the graph near the asymptote. Graphing utilities differ in the way they plot values near asymptotes. Some graphing utilities falsely join points across asymptotes. The visual picture may not be what you expect!

Weather balloon take-offs

The model used is based on the notion of an upper limit in the height that a weather balloon can reach.

A good way of tackling question **4c** is to draw the horizontal line $h = 9990$ and find out where this line intersects the graph of the balloon's height function.

Farm fields

The set of x values on which a function f is defined is called the *domain*, and the set of y values which the function takes is its *range*. Unfortunately, many graphing utilities use the term "range" loosely, including using it instead of domain. We have tried to be precise. If this is the first time students are asked to graph a function with a restricted domain, consult the section "How to restrict the domain of a function" in the appropriate appendix or use your graphing utility manual.

A good way to do question 5 is to find the intersection of the graph with the line $d = w$.

Answers

Sharing chocolates (page 59)

1 a $(1, 36), (3, 12), (8, 4.5), (24, 1.5), (72, 0.5), (144, 0.25)$

  c choosing an appropriate scale

2 a Divide 36 by n; $C(n) = \dfrac{36}{n}$

  c positive integers; positive fractions

3 a 0.049   **b** Zoom in around graph at $x = 1,000,000$.

4 a yes; $(6, 6)$ **b** Find intersection of $y = \dfrac{36}{n}$ and $y = n$.

Weather balloon take-offs (page 61)

1 first 10 minutes

2 last 10 minutes

3 a 9,945 meters   **b** 9,944.75 meters

4 a Balloon gets closer to a height of 10,000 meters.

  b As t gets larger, the second term gets closer to zero.

  c after 999 seconds

Farm fields (page 62)

1 $d = \dfrac{20\ 000}{w}$

2 100 meters

3 400 meters

4 317. 5 meters

5 141.42 meters by 141.42 meters

6 a 50 meters   **b** 400 meters   **c** $50 \le w \le 400$

7 end points—$f(w)$: $(50, 800), (400, 100)$; $g(w)$: $(50, 100), (400, 800)$; $P(w)$: $(50, 900)$, $(400, 900)$

8 400; 200; 600; $P(100) = f(100) + g(100)$

9 a 141.4 meters   **b** 565.7 meters

  c 141.4 meters $\times$ 141.4 meters (a square!)

10 $(141.4, 282.8)$; first coordinate gives the same answer as question 9a, second coordinate is one half of the answers to question 9b.

Scuba diving (page 64)

1 See table below.

Depth (*D*) in meters	0	10	20	30	40	50	60
Pressure (*P*) in atmospheres	1	2	3	4	5	6	7
Volume (*V*) of air in lungs in liters	4	2	$\frac{4}{3}$	1	$\frac{4}{5}$	$\frac{2}{3}$	$\frac{4}{7}$

2 a See table below.

Depth (*D*) in meters	0	10	20	30	40	50	60
Pressure (*P*) in atmospheres	1	2	3	4	5	6	7
Volume (*V*) of air in lungs in liters	28	14	$\frac{28}{3}$	7	$\frac{28}{5}$	$\frac{14}{3}$	4

b $P = \dfrac{D + 10}{10}$ **c** $V = \dfrac{28}{P}$ **e** near the surface

Transformation Creations on Families of Reciprocal Functions

Aims

In this section students will:

- see how changing constants in a reciprocal function rule affects the shape and position of a hyperbola graph;
- learn how to translate hyperbolas to the left and right;
- learn how to translate hyperbolas up and down;
- find how the algebraic equation of a hyperbola relates to the asymptotes of the hyperbola.

Creations

Some teachers may like to use "creations" to explore properties of the function families. Others may wish to use them to revise properties. For each creation, the boundaries indicated are only a guide, and students should not waste time attempting to perfect the viewing window dimensions. To set the viewing window for each creation, consult the section "Changing the viewing window" in the appropriate appendix or use your graphing utility manual.

The quickest way to enter the dimension of the viewing window for the graphing utilities in the appendices is:

- *CFX-9850G*—press SHIFT and **F3** (**V-Window**) and enter the viewing window dimensions.
- *HP 38G*—press the blue key and PLOT and enter the viewing window dimensions.
- *TI-82/83*—press the WINDOW key and enter the viewing window dimensions.

Student designs will differ slightly from those illustrated in the book, while retaining the essential features. The features that should be correct are written in the description. It is not necessary that students attempt every creation.

You will need to show students how to plot families of functions. Consult the section "How to plot a family of functions" in the appropriate appendix or use your graphing utility manual.

Answers

Creations (page 66)

1 *Hug me:* $y = \dfrac{1}{x}, y = \dfrac{1}{2-x}$ **2** *Cross:* $y = \pm\dfrac{1}{x}, \pm\dfrac{2}{x}, \pm\dfrac{3}{x}$

3 *Across a cross:* $y = \pm x, y = \pm\dfrac{2}{x}, y = \pm\dfrac{2.5}{x}$

4 *Waterfall:* $y = \dfrac{1}{x} \pm 3, y = \dfrac{1}{x} \pm 2, y = \dfrac{1}{x} \pm 1, y = \dfrac{1}{x} + 4, y = \dfrac{1}{x}$

5 *Elbows:* $y = \dfrac{1}{x}, y = \dfrac{1}{x-2} + 2$

6 *Fish kiss:* $y = \dfrac{1}{x-1}, y = \dfrac{1}{x-1} + 1, y = \dfrac{1}{x} + 1, y = \dfrac{1}{x+1}, y = \dfrac{1}{x+1} - 1, y = \dfrac{1}{x} - 1, y = \dfrac{1}{x}$

Reciprocal function graphs and constants (page 70)

1 It stretches the graph in the vertical direction, and so affects how far the two branches are apart.

2 Translates or moves the graph of $y = \dfrac{1}{x}$ by h units to the right $(h > 0)$ or left $(h < 0)$.

3 Translates or moves graph of $y = \dfrac{1}{x}$ by k units up $(k > 0)$ or down $(k < 0)$.

4 Intersection point of the horizontal and vertical asymptotes.

The Big Picture

Aims

In this section students will:

- use zooming to get a big picture of the graph of a function;
- see that the graphs of exponential and reciprocal functions change very rapidly;
- use the big picture to find all the intersections of pairs of function graphs.

Answers (page 72)

The answers for questions **1** to **10** show the intercepts and the graphs.

1 $(0,0)$ **2** $(0, 0.81)$ **3** $(0, 11)$

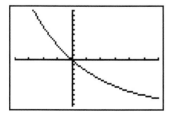 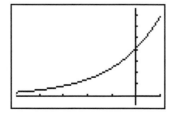 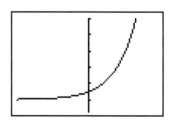

4 $(0, 1)$ and $(7.27, 0)$

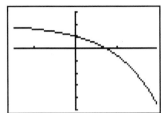

5 $(0, 24.8)$ and $(11.9, 0)$

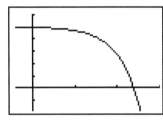

6 $(0.04, 0)$; asymptotes are $x = 0$ and $y = 25$.

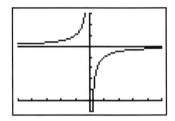

7 $(0, -1)$; asymptotes are $x = 0.01$ and $y = 0$.

 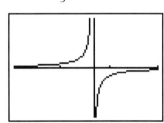

8 $(0, 0.01)$; asymptotes are $x = 33\frac{1}{3}$ and $y = 0$.

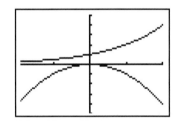

9 $(0, 1)$ and $(10, 0)$. $x = -10$ and $y = -1$.

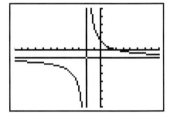

10 a No solution (exponential function always positive, parabola always negative or zero)

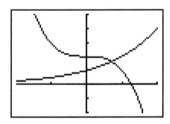

b $(0.712, 1.64)$

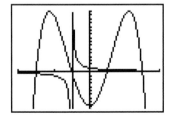

c $(3.43, 250)$

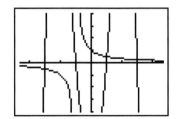

d $(1.03, 0.492)$, $(2.99, 0.250)$, $(-3.01, -0.497)$

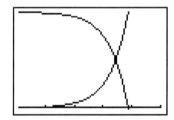

The Rubber Sheet

Aims

In this section students will:

- see how the graph of a function can look very different in different viewing windows;
- learn how to give a deceptive picture of a function;
- find that not all features of a graph can be changed by changing the viewing window;
- learn that exponential functions eventually increase faster than quadratic functions.

Comparing function families

Question 1 is designed to show students that an exponential graph rises very rapidly yet has no vertical asymptote—it does, however, have a horizontal asymptote. Question 2 is designed to show students that a reciprocal function graph rises more rapidly than an exponential function near its vertical asymptote. Question 3 is designed to show students that exponential functions eventually increase more rapidly than quadratic functions.

Answers (page 73)

1 a *Hint:* a small viewing window around the origin.
  b *Hint:* a large window around $(500, -1)$.
  c *Hint:* a large window around $(45, -0.9)$.

2 a *Hint:* a large viewing window at first, shrinking the x-axis a number of times.
  b *Hint:* a small viewing window around the point $(-32, 1.95)$.

3 a *Hint:* a small viewing window around the point $(0.13, 0.09)$.
  b *Hint:* a small viewing window around the point $(0.1, 0.098)$.
  c *Hint:* a small viewing window around the origin.

4 a *Hint:* a small viewing window around the point $(0.04, 0)$.
  b *Hint:* a small viewing window around the point $(-0.03, 55)$.

6 a no   **b** no   **c** yes

Comparing function families (page 76)

1 a No, since no matter what value of x we choose, there is always a value of y, however large; no vertical asymptotes.
  b Yes, since 2^x is always greater than zero; $y = 0$ or $y = $ (any negative number).

2 a i no   **ii** yes
  b Yes; $x = 1$; they have one vertical asymptote.
  c Yes; $y = {}^-1$, the horizontal asymptote.
  d Reciprocal functions have both horizontal and vertical asymptotes.

3 a If the value of a is small enough, the exponential graph may lie above the parabola (see **b**).
  b yes, if $a < 0.8875$
  c i yes (a tangent to the exponential curve when $a \approx 0.8875$)
    ii yes, if $a > 0.8875$ **iii** no

Appendix B
Working with the CFX-9850G

CFX-9850G QUICK START!

This "Quick Start" page describes the five steps necessary to enter and plot a function with the CFX-9850G, using the example function $f(x) = 2x - 3$. A more detailed set of instructions for entering and plotting functions can be found in the next section of this appendix.

Five "Quick Start" steps to enter and plot a function

Step 1   To turn the CFX-9850G on, press **AC/ON** and then press **5** to enter the GRAPH mode.

Step 2   Press the keys required to create a function rule. To represent the independent variable X, the CFX-9850G uses the variable key **X,θ,T**. In this example, type in the function $Y_1 = 2x - 3$ by pressing the following sequence of keys.

Step 3   Press **SHIFT** and then **F3** (**V-Window**); then press **F1** (**INIT**). This creates the default viewing window, which is $-6.3 \leq x \leq 6.3$ and $-3.1 \leq y \leq 3.1$.

Step 4   Press **EXIT** and then **F6** (**DRAW**) to view the graph of the function you have entered.

Step 5   Press **F1** (**Trace**). This locates the cursor on the graph of the function Y_1, allowing the user to trace the function along the path of Y_1. The equation is displayed in the top left hand corner of the screen to indicate which function's coordinates are being displayed (see diagram below). Use the **left** and **right cursor** keys to "trace" the path of the function. The coordinates of the cursor are updated each time the cursor keys are pressed.

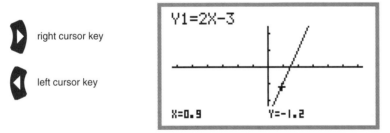

*The **left** and **right cursor** keys and the graph of $Y_1 = 2x - 3$ with the*
***Trace** option activated to display graph coordinates*

GETTING STARTED WITH THE CFX-9850G

About the CFX-9850G

The CFX-9850G is made by Casio Corporation and is available through your local calculator dealer. This appendix is not intended to be a product manual, but rather a convenient collection of "How to ..." descriptions of the procedures that are needed to complete all tasks within this book. Teachers are strongly advised to familiarize themselves with all the features of the graphics calculator in this appendix.

101

Managing a work session

How to turn the CFX-9850G on/off

- To turn the CFX-9850G on, press **AC/ON**.

- To turn the CFX-9850G off, press **SHIFT** and then **AC/ON** (Note that the **SHIFT** function **OFF** is printed above the key in yellow.)

Note: The CFX-9850G has an automatic "shutdown" feature which powers the CFX-9850G down after a few minutes. However, the contents of the display are saved for when it is next turned on. This means that any functions entered, graphs plotted and changes to the viewing window dimensions are still in the calculator's memory. It is important to be aware of this and wise to establish a routine of "clearing" any existing functions and returning to the default viewing window before starting on a new activity. "Resetting" the calculator involves deleting all data (including any programs) and restoring all default settings.

How to clear all existing information

Often you wish to begin a work session by clearing all previously entered information. To achieve this, perform the following steps.

Step 1   After turning the calculator on, use the cursor keys to select the **MEM** icon.

Step 2   Press **EXE** to enter the **MEM** mode (for memory management).

Step 3   Use the **down cursor** key to select the **Reset** option, and then press **EXE**.

Step 4   Press **F1** (**YES**) to confirm that you wish to reset all memories.

Step 5   Press **MENU** to return to the icon menu.

Entering and plotting functions

With the CFX-9850G, the rules for functions are entered via the calculator keys. A maximum of 20 functions may be entered concurrently. The notation used to define each function is the Y_n format, where n is an integer between 1 to 20 inclusive.

How to enter and plot a function

Step 1   Press **MENU**, and then press **5** to enter **GRAPH** mode (for working with function rules and graphs).
The following screen should appear. Note that the screen can fit six function rules. There are, in fact, 20 function definitions permitted, but the others are off screen and can be accessed with the down cursor key.

Step 2   Press the keys required to create a function rule. To represent the independent variable X, press the variable key **X,θ,T**. In this example, type in the function $Y_1 = x^2 + 3x + 2$ by pressing the following sequence of keys:

The Function definition screen on the CFX-9850G

If you have made errors when entering the function (for example, wrong symbol), use the cursor keys to return to the location of the incorrect symbol, and press the correct keys. This should replace the old symbol with the new correct one.

Step 3   Press **SHIFT** and then **F3** (**V-Window**). Then press **F1** (INIT) to return to the default viewing window.

Step 4   Press **EXIT** to return to the function rule screen and then press **F6** (DRAW) and the graph below will appear.

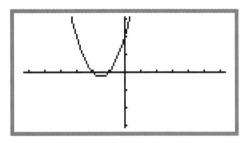

The graph of the function $Y_1 = x^2 + 3x + 2$ plotted on the CFX-9850G

How to enter and plot more than one function

If you wish to enter and plot a number of functions on the same set of axes, follow the steps below.

Step 1   Enter the first function as described previously in the section entitled "How to enter and plot a function."

Step 2   To enter further functions, press **F6** (G↔T) to move to the function rule screen.

Step 3   Move the cursor to the next empty function rule line.

Step 4   Type the appropriate keys to enter the desired functions.

Step 5   Repeat steps 3 and 4 until all functions have been entered.

Step 6   Press **F6** (DRAW) to display the graphs of all entered functions.

How to enter and plot a function using parameters

It is possible to change the rule and re-plot a function without editing a function directly. To do this it is possible to enter a function rule including parameters (constants). For example, we can enter a function of the form $y = A(x - 2)^2 + 1$, where A is the parameter. By assigning different values for A, we are able to change the function rule and its associated graph without re-entering the function rule.

Step 1   Press **MENU** to access the icon menu.

Step 2   Press **5** to enter **GRAPH** mode.

Step 3   Clear any existing function rules by pressing **F2** (**DEL**) and **F1** (**YES**) and then press the required keys to complete entering the rule, $Y_1 = A(X - 2)^2 + 1$, $[A = -1, 1, 3]$.

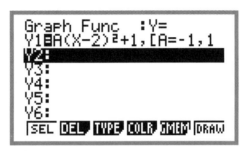

Function definition screen showing a rule using three values
for the parameter A (not all visible)

Step 4   Press **EXE** to store the functions.

Step 5   Press **F6** (**DRAW**) to plot the graph of the functions.

Note: To enter the parameter A, press **ALPHA**, followed by **X,θ,T** which has the red **A** character printed above the key on the right.

To enter the **[** symbol, press **SHIFT**, followed by **+** which has the yellow **[** symbol printed above the key on the left.

To enter the **]** symbol, press **SHIFT**, followed by **−** which has the yellow **]** symbol printed above the key on the left.

To enter the **=** symbol, press **SHIFT**, followed by **·** which has the yellow **=** symbol printed above the key on the left.

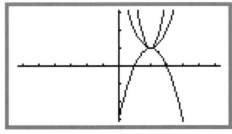

Graph screen showing the graphs of Y_1 for the three values listed for the parameter A

How to plot a family of functions

A family of functions is a set of functions that are identical except for the value of a particular constant. For example, $f(x) = x^2 - 2$, $f(x) = x^2$ and $f(x) = x^2 + 2$ are all member functions of a family, written as $f(x) = x^2 + a$. With a CFX-9850G, we can work with a family of functions by following the next procedure.

In this example the function family will be of the form $Y_1 = x^2 + a$, where $a = \{-2, 0, 2\}$.

Step 1   Press MENU to access the icon menu.

Step 2   Press 5 to enter **GRAPH** mode.

Step 3   Clear any existing rules and then enter the rule for the function $Y_1 = x^2 + a$ by entering the following sequence:

Step 4   Press EXE to store the functions.

Step 5   Press F6 (**DRAW**) to plot the graph of the functions.

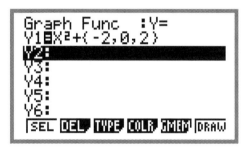

Defining a function with changeable constants.
This creates the three graphs $y = x^2 - 2$, $y = x^2$ and $y = x^2 + 2$

The graph of $f(x) = x^2 + a$ will be plotted for $a = -2$, 0 and 2 (see resultant graphs below). The method of data entry shown in the above example is very useful for quickly observing the impact of a particular constant on the shape of a graph.

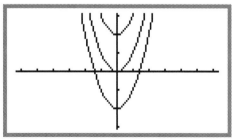

The family of functions of the form $f(x) = x^2 + a$ for $a = -2$, 0 and 2

How to restrict the domain of a function

The set of x values for which the function is defined is called the domain of the function. Let us say, for example, that a function $f(x) = x^2$ is only defined for $-1 \leq x \leq 1.5$. It is possible for the CFX-9850G to incorporate this restriction by following the procedure listed below.

Step 1   Press **MENU** to access the icon menu.

Step 2   Press **5** to enter **GRAPH** mode.

Step 3   Clear any existing rules and then press the appropriate keys to enter the function:
$$Y_1 = x^2, \ [-1,1.5]$$

Step 4   Press **EXE** to store the function rule.

Step 5   Press **F6** (**DRAW**) to plot the graph of the function with a restricted domain.

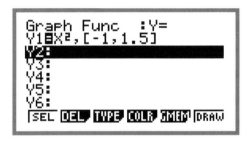

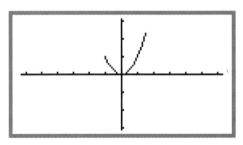

Defining (and graphing) the function $y = x^2$ with a restricted domain of $-1 \leq x \leq 1.5$

After pressing **F6** (**DRAW**), the graph of $f(x)$ should now appear, incorporating the restricted values for x. Note how the function is only plotted between $x = -1$ and $x = 1.5$. This procedure of restricting the function is very useful in modeling as it allows us to focus on the x values (domain) for which a rule makes sense.

Entering brackets, exponents and fractions

The syntax rules on the CFX-9850G strictly follow the normal rules for the order of mathematical operations (for example, brackets, exponents, division and multiplication, then addition and subtraction). A function rule, when defined, occupies a single line and therefore can be hard to read. For example, an expression such as:
$$Y_2 = \frac{x-3}{x+2}$$
will appear on screen as **Y2 =(X–3)/(X+2)**.

When entering function rules, pay careful attention to the order of operations. When in doubt, use brackets to make your intention clear.

How to enter brackets

Step 1   Press ▮**(** to open the brackets.

Step 2   Enter any symbols/terms that should be within the brackets.

Step 3   Press ▮**)** to close the brackets.

How to enter exponents (powers)

● If the exponent is 2 (that is, for x^2) press **X,θ,T** followed by **x^2** .

● If the exponent is −1 (that is, for x^{-1}) press **X,θ,T** followed by **SHIFT** **)** (x^{-1}).

● If the exponent is a number other than 2 or −1, (for example, x^3) press **X,θ,T** followed by **∧** followed by the exponent (for example, 3).

● If the exponent is not a single term (for example, 2^{x+3}) make sure that you bracket the terms that are exponents (for example, **2^(X+3)**).

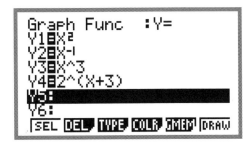

Some examples of the syntax displayed when entering exponents on a CFX-9850G

How to enter fractions

Step 1   For simple fractions, press the keys for the numerator.

Step 2   Press **÷** (it will appear as ÷ on the screen).

Step 3   Press the keys for the denominator.

For more complicated fractions (involving more than one term in either the numerator or denominator or both), ensure that you use brackets to preserve the order of operations. Some examples are shown.

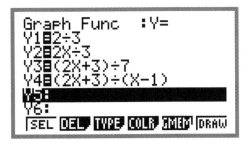

Some examples of the appropriate use of fractions and brackets when entering function rules

Clearing function rules and graphs

How to clear a function rule and its graph

Step 1   Press **MENU** to access the icon menu.

Step 2   Press **5** to enter **GRAPH** mode. This will bring all defined function rules into view.

Step 3   Use the cursor keys to move to the function rule you wish to clear.

Step 4   Press **F2** (**DEL**) and then **F1** (**YES**) to clear the rule.

Step 5   Repeat steps 3 and 4 to clear any other function rules and their graphs.

See also "How to stop the CFX-9850G from plotting a graph" in the next section.

WORKING WITH FUNCTION GRAPHS ON THE CFX-9850G

Working with the graph window

How to display graph coordinates

Step 1   Press **MENU** to access the icon menu.

Step 2   Press **5** to enter **GRAPH** mode. This will bring all defined function rules into view.

Step 3   Press **F6** (**DRAW**) (this step assumes that you have already entered a function rule).

Step 4   Press **F1** (**Trace**). This locates the cursor on the graph of the function Y_1, allowing the user to trace the function along the path of Y_1. The function rule is displayed in the top left-hand corner of the screen to indicate the function whose coordinates are being displayed (see the diagram on the next page).

Step 5   Use the **left** and **right cursor** keys to trace the path of the function. The coordinates of the cursor are updated each time the cursor keys are pressed.

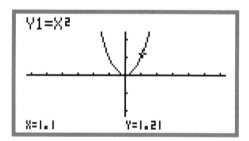

*The graph of $Y_1 = x^2$ with the **Trace** option activated to display graph coordinates*

Step 6   If you wish to trace the function Y_2, Y_3 or another function graph that you have defined, press the down cursor key to move the cursor to the other function graphs. The rule will be displayed in the top left-hand corner of the screen (as shown below) indicating which function graph's coordinates are currently being displayed.

Step 7   Use the **left** and **right cursor** keys to trace the path of the function. The coordinates of the cursor are updated each time the cursor keys are pressed.

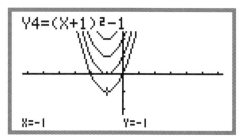

*Using the **Trace** and cursor keys to display the coordinates of Y_4*

How to stop the CFX-9850G from plotting a graph

Each time a new function is defined in the **Y=** screen, the CFX-9850G assumes you will want to graph it, so if you press **F6** (**DRAW**), the calculator will attempt to plot the new function.

If you wish to prevent the CFX-9850G from plotting any function, follow the next procedure (assumes you have a function entered in Y_1).

Step 1   Press **F6** (**G↔T**) to toggle to the function definition screen (if not already displayed).

Step 2   Locate the cursor on the function whose graph you wish to prevent being plotted (Y_1 here). Note that the = symbol for Y_1 is blackened. This means that this function is "selected," and will be plotted.

Step 3   Press **F1** (**SEL**). This de-selects the function, and removes the blackened background. It will now not plot the function Y_1.

Confirm that this disables graphing the current function by pressing **F6**.

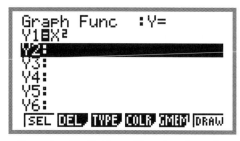

Function Y_1 "selected" to be plotted

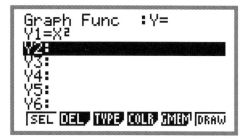

Function Y_1 "de-selected" not to be plotted

Step 4   To re-plot a "de-selected" function, repeat the process to "select" the function again.

109

How to display the function rule and graph simultaneously

Once the function has been plotted, it is possible to display its associated rule by following these steps.

Step 1   Press **F6** (DRAW) (this step assumes that you have already entered a function rule).

Step 2   Press **F1** (**Trace**). This locates the cursor on the graph of the function Y_1, with the associated function rule displayed in the top left of the screen.

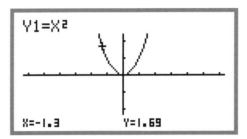

*Using the **Trace** feature to view both the function rule and its graph simultaneously*

Changing the viewing window

The Graph screen can be thought of as a true "window" through which we can observe the graphs of defined functions. If the relevant portion(s) of the function's graph are not quite in view, there are a number of options for changing the viewing window so that we can more clearly examine the behavior of the function.

How to change to the default viewing window

Step 1   Press **SHIFT**, then **F3** (**V-Window**). (Assumes you are in the graph screen or the function definition screen.)

Step 2   Press **F1** (INIT). This creates the default viewing window dimensions, which are $-6.3 \le x \le 6.3$ and $-3.1 \le y \le 3.1$.

Step 3   Press **EXIT** and then **F6** (DRAW) to display the graph screen.

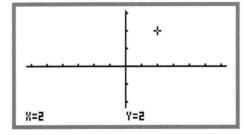

The default viewing window for the CFX-9850G
(is $-6.3 \le x \le 6.3$ and $-3.1 \le y \le 3.1$)

How to specify the viewing window dimensions

Step 1   Press **SHIFT**, then **F3** (**V-Window**). (Assumes you are in the graph screen or the function definition screen.) This will bring up the screen shown below.

Changing the viewing window by using the V-Window key

Step 2   Use the **up** and **down cursor** keys to move to the **View Window** option you wish to alter. Then enter the new figure. The available options are explained below.

Xmin/Xmax—the minimum/maximum x value that will be visible in the viewing window.

Ymin/Ymax—the minimum/maximum y value that will be visible in the window.

Xscale/Yscale—the number of units between markings on the x-axis and y-axis.

Step 3   Press **EXIT** then **F6** (**DRAW**) to show the resultant change in the viewing window.

How to locate a graph not visible in the current viewing window

Sometimes the graph may not be displayed in the current viewing window. The Casio CFX-9850G has a feature which adjusts the Ymin and Ymax values so that the graph of the function comes into view (for the current x values).

Step 1   Press the required keys to enter the rule $Y_1 = x^2 + 12$.

Step 2   Press **SHIFT**, then **F3** (**V-Window**).

Step 3   Press **F1** (**INIT**) to select the default viewing window.

Step 4   Press **EXIT** and then **F6** (**DRAW**) to display the graph screen.
          Note that the graph is not in view.

Step 5   Press **F2** (**Zoom**) and then **F5** (**AUTO**) to "locate" the graph for the current x values.

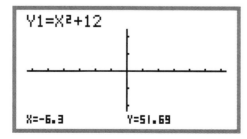

The default viewing window is shown above

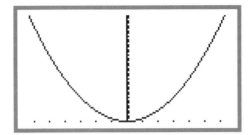

*Using the **Zoom** AUTO feature to create a better view of the previous graph*

How to change the center of the viewing window

The cursor keys allow the user to make slight adjustments to the viewing window so that a relevant part of the graph may come into view.

Step 1   Press the required keys to enter the rule $Y_1 = x^2 - 4$.

Step 2   Press SHIFT, then F3 (**V-Window**).

Step 3   Press F1 (INIT) to select the default viewing window.

Step 4   Press EXIT and then F6 (DRAW) to display the graph screen.
         Note that the vertex or turning point of the parabola is not in view.

Step 5   Press the **down cursor** key to move the viewing window down slightly, revealing the location of the vertex. Note that each time you press the cursor keys, the viewing window moves slightly in the direction of that cursor key.

Using scaling/zooming options

Scaling is the process of changing the scales on either or both axes. Graphing calculators often refer to the process of zooming in and zooming out:

● **zooming in**—looking more closely at the graph through a smaller viewing window;

● **zooming out**—looking more widely at the graph through a larger viewing window.

Zooming in permits the user to focus more precisely on a portion of the graph. With the CFX-9850G, there are three main ways to zoom in:

● Use the **V-Window** option to make the viewing window include a smaller region of the X–Y plane (see previous section).

● Use **Zoom** and the IN option to select a new viewing window center point and zoom in around that point.

● Use the **Zoom** and the BOX option to select and zoom in to a "boxed" region within the current viewing window.

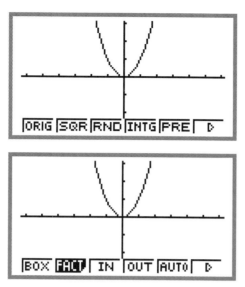

*The options available after pressing **F2**(**Zoom**)*

How to return to the default zoom level

Step 1   Press SHIFT, then **F3** (**V-Window**). (Assumes you are in the graph screen or the function definition screen.)

Step 2   Press **F1** (**INIT**). This creates the default viewing window dimensions which are $-6.3 \leq x \leq 6.3$ and $-3.1 \leq y \leq 3.1$.

Step 3   Press **EXIT** and then **F6** (**DRAW**) to display the graph screen.

How to zoom in with the IN option

Zoom and the **IN** option permit zooming in, based on the current viewing window. The CFX-9850G defaults to zooming in on both axes by a factor of two.

Step 1   Press the required keys to enter the rule $Y_1 = x^2$

Step 2   Press SHIFT, then **F3** (**V-Window**). (Assumes you are in the graph screen or the function definition screen.)

Step 3   Press **F1** (**INIT**). This creates the default viewing window, which is $-6.3 \leq x \leq 6.3$ and $-3.1 \leq y \leq 3.1$.

Step 4   Press **EXIT** and then **F6** (**DRAW**) to display the graph screen.

Step 5   Press **F2** (**Zoom**) and then **F3** (**IN**) to zoom in by a factor of two.

Step 6   To zoom in further, press **F3** (**IN**) again.

   Note: Each use of **Zoom-IN** halves the value of $X_{max} - X_{min}$ as well as the value of $Y_{max} - Y_{min}$.

How to box zoom with the BOX option

Zoom and the **BOX** option permits zooming inside a user definable rectangular "box" of the current viewing window. This box becomes the new viewing window.

Step 1   Press the required keys to enter the rule $Y_1 = x^2$.

Step 2   Press **SHIFT**, then **F3** (**V-Window**). (Assumes you are in the graph screen or the function definition screen.)

Step 3   Press **F1** (**INIT**). This creates the default viewing window, which is $-6.3 \leq x \leq 6.3$ and $-3.1 \leq y \leq 3.1$.

Step 4   Press **EXIT** and then **F6** (**DRAW**) to display the graph screen.

Step 5   Press **F2** (**Zoom**) and then **F1** (**BOX**) to zoom in by a factor of two.

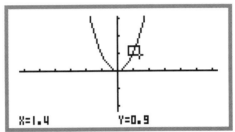

*Zooming in using the **Zoom-BOX** option. Note the box that has been defined.*

Step 6   Use the cursor keys to locate the upper left corner of the zoom box.

Step 7   Press **EXE**.

Step 8   Use the cursor keys to locate the bottom right corner of the zoom box (a box will be created on screen).

Step 9   Press **EXE**. (This then zooms into the boxed region.)

How to zoom out with the OUT option

Zooming out permits the user to observe more of the graph, including perhaps more of the general shape or global features of the graph. The CFX-9850G defaults to zooming out on both axes by a factor of two.

Step 1   Press the required keys to enter the rule $Y_1 = x^2$.

Step 2   Press **SHIFT**, then **F3** (**V-Window**). (Assumes you are in the graph screen or the function definition screen.)

Step 3   Press **F1** (**INIT**). This creates the default viewing window, which is $-6.3 \leq x \leq 6.3$ and $-3.1 \leq y \leq 3.1$.

Step 4   Press **EXIT** and then **F6** (**DRAW**) to display the graph screen.

Step 5   Press **F2** (**Zoom**) and then **F4** (**OUT**) to zoom out by a factor of two.

Step 6   To zoom out further, press **F4** (**OUT**) again.

Note: Each use of **Zoom-OUT** doubles the value of $X_{max} - X_{min}$ as well as the value of $Y_{max} - Y_{min}$.

How to use the PRE option

Zoom and the PRE option permit the user to return to the previous zoom level. This is particularly useful if you have chosen an inappropriate viewing window, and wish to return to the previous viewing window you were using.

Step 1   Press **F2** (**Zoom**) and then **F6** (**MORE**) to view the other zoom options.

Step 2   Press **F5** (**PRE**) to return to the previous zoom setting (or viewing window)

Note: The Casio CFX-9850G also has a **Zoom-ORIG**, which re-creates the original viewing window used before any zoom steps were performed.

How to use the SQR option

The SQR option on the **Zoom** screen attempts to display the true graph proportions by replotting the graphs of all entered functions with equal scales for the x- and y-axes. It does this by altering the current viewing window so that pressing the left or right cursor key moves the cursor the same distance as pressing the up or down cursor key.

Step 1   Press the required keys to enter the rule $Y_1 = x$.

Step 2   Press **SHIFT**, then **F3** (**V-Window**). (Assumes you are in the graph screen or the function definition screen.)

Step 3   Press **F3** (**STD**). This creates the standard viewing window, which is $-10 \le x \le 10$ and $-10 \le y \le 10$.

Step 4   Press **EXIT** and then **F6** (**DRAW**) to display the graph screen.

Note: The linear graph should be at 45° with respect to the x-axis, but is not. Note also how the axis markings on the y-axis are differently spaced to those on the x-axis.

Step 5   Press **F2** (**Zoom**) and then **F6** (**MORE**) to view the other zoom options.

Step 6   Press **F2** (**SQR**) to create a viewing window in which true proportions are displayed. (It will also create axis markings that have equivalent spacing on each axis.)

How to change the zoom factors

The default zoom factor is two for each axis. This means that zooming in (or out) creates a change in the magnification of 200% in the direction of each axis. The procedure for changing any or all of these zoom factors is given below.

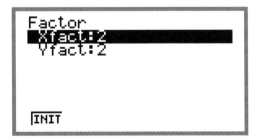

*The **Factor** option (for changing the zoom factors)*

115

Step 1   Press **F2** (**Zoom**) and then **F2** (FACT) to view the zoom factors editing screen.

Step 2   Change the values of **Xfact** or **Yfact** as required.

Step 3   Press **EXIT** to return to the graph screen.

WORKING WITH ADDITIONAL FEATURES ON THE CFX-9850G

Creating a table of function values

Creating a table of values from the function provides another representation of the function. It could be convenient for listing the function values of a number of functions at once. The next example creates a table of values for the function $f(x) = x^2$ for $23 \leq x \leq 25$, with increments of 0.1.

How to create a table of values

Step 1   Press **MENU** and then press **7** to enter TABLE mode.

Step 2   Press the required keys to enter the rule $Y_1 = x^2$.

Step 3   Press **F5** (RANG) to enter table parameters.

Step 4   Enter 23 as the new **Start** (minimum x value for table).

Step 5   Enter 25 as the new **End** (maximum x value for table).

Step 6   Enter 0.1 as the new **Pitch** (x increment for table).

*Setting the **Table** options*

Step 7   Press **EXIT** and then press **F6** (TABL) to view the table of function values. The result is shown below.

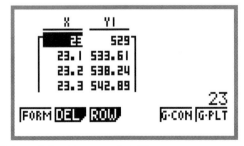

Sample table for $f(x) = x^2$ for $23 \leq x \leq 25$ (for increments in the X values of 0.1)

Step 8   Use the cursor keys to scroll down through the list.

Plotting points

When attempting to fit functions to data that has been collected, it is convenient to plot data points, and then attempt to find function graphs which seem to line up with the points. The sample chart below illustrates a possible scenario where plotting points might be used.

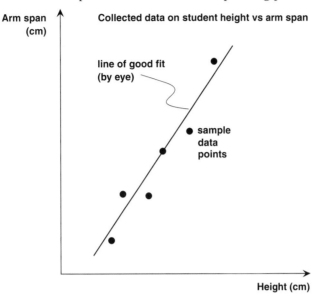

How to change the display precision

When entering data, it is useful to set the display precision first so that the data is displayed with the appropriate number of decimal points.

Step 1   Press **MENU** and then press **2** to enter **STAT** mode.

Step 2   Press **SHIFT** and then **MENU** to enter **SET UP** options.

Step 3   Use the down cursor key until you have located it on the line marked **Display**.

Step 4   Press the appropriate function keys (**F1–F6**) to select either a fixed display precision (**Fix**) of 0–9 decimal points, or floating precision (**Norm**) to allow the CFX-9850G to select the display precision dependent on the figures entered and calculations performed.

Using the STAT SET UP screen to change the display precision

How to plot points

In this example, use the following data values.

x	1	2	3	4	5	6
y	2.2	3.5	4.7	6.6	7.2	9.1

Step 1   Press MENU and then press 2 to enter STAT mode.

If points are already listed in a column, you may clear them by moving the cursor to the head of the column (for example, List 1) and pressing F6 (MORE), F4 (DEL·A) and then F1 (YES) to confirm.

Step 2   Enter the x values above into the column L1. Press EXE after each entry.

Step 3   Enter the y values above into the column L2. Press EXE after each entry.

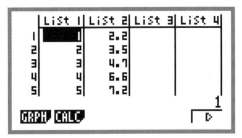

Table of values for x and y shown in the STAT-List screen

Step 4   Press F1 (GRPH) to get the Stat plots main menu at the bottom of the screen.

Step 5   Press F6 (SET) to indicate that you wish to set up a plot.

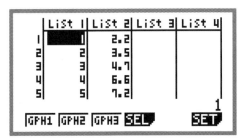

The Stat plots main menu for defining statistical plot options

Step 6   Use the cursor keys and the keys F1–F6 to set the options as shown in this diagram.

Setting statistical plot options for StatGraph1

Step 7 Press **EXIT** to return to the **STAT-List** window.

Step 8 Press **F1** (**GPH1**). This will plot and display the data points for **StatGraph1** in an appropriate viewing window.

Note: The keys **F1–F6** here are for overlaying regression lines, which is not covered here.

Step 9 Press **SHIFT** and **F1** (**Trace**). Using the **right** and **left cursor** keys allows you to observe the coordinates of each point.

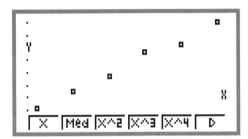

A scatter plot of the above data plotted on the CFX-9850G **STAT-Graph** *screen*

How to fit a function to data by eye

It is possible to try different functions that might fit the data points. One useful way of constructing such functions on the CFX-9850G is to use the **Sketch** function. In this example (using the data entered and plotted above), we will try to fit a function of the form $y = Ax$, where A is the parameter that we will alter to try to achieve a good fit.

Step 1 Press **MENU** and then press **1** to enter **RUN** mode.

Step 2 Press **SHIFT** and then **F4** (**Sketch**) to indicate that you wish to "draw" an object over the data.

Step 3 Press **F5** (**GRPH**) and then **F1** (**Y=**) to indicate that a function graph is to be drawn over the data.

Step 4 Press **1** **·** **4** and then **X,θ,T** to indicate that you wish to plot the graph of $y = 1.4x$ over the data.

The **RUN** *screen showing the rule of the graph which will overlay the data*

119

Step 5 Press 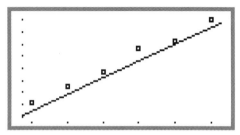 to observe if the value of $A = 1.4$ gave a "good fit" for the data set present.

The Graph screen after parameter A has been set to 1.4

To try other values of A:

Step 6 Press **F6** (G↔T) key to "toggle" back to the text screen.

Step 7 Press the left cursor key, and then edit the function rule.

Step 8 Press 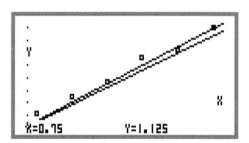 to plot the new function on top of previous ones.

The STAT Graph screen after parameter A has been adjusted from 1.4 to 1.5

Note: The **Trace** option only works for the last function drawn. Also, to clear any drawn graphs, press SHIFT **F4** (**Sketch**) **F1** (**Cls**) and EXE.

Appendix C
Working with the HP 38G

HP 38G QUICK START!

This "Quick Start" page describes the five steps necessary to enter and plot a function with the HP 38G, using the example function $f(x) = 2x - 3$. A more detailed set of instructions for entering and plotting functions can be found in the next section of this appendix.

Five "Quick Start" steps to enter and plot a function

Step 1   To turn the HP 38G on, press **ON** and then press **LIB** (to access the aplet library).

Step 2   Move to highlight **Function** with the **up** and **down cursor** keys, ▲ and ▼.
Press ▓ the second black key from the left below the menu word **RESET** at the bottom of the screen, and then press the black menu key below **YES** (to confirm).
This resets all the default options for the **Function** aplet, including setting the viewing window dimensions to $-6.5 \le x \le 6.5$ and $-3.1 \le y \le 3.2$.

Step 3   Press below **START** to launch the **Function** aplet. Press the keys required to create a function rule. To represent the independent variable x, the HP 38G uses the variable key **X,T,θ**. In this example, type in the function $F_1(x) = 2x - 3$ by pressing the following sequence of keys.

2 **X,T,θ** **−** **3** **ENTER**

Step 4   Press **PLOT** to view the graph of the function you have entered.

Step 5   Press the **right cursor** key to locate the cursor on the graph of the function $F_1(x)$, allowing the user to trace the function along the path of $F_1(x)$. The value **F1(X): 1.4** displayed in the center of the screen below the graph indicates that $F_1(x)$ is the function whose coordinates are being displayed (see diagram below). Use the **left** and **right cursor** keys to trace the path of the function. The coordinates of the cursor are updated each time the cursor keys are pressed.

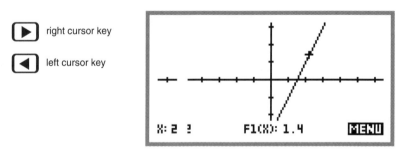

▶ right cursor key

◀ left cursor key

X: 2 ?   F1(X): 1.4   MENU

*The **left** and **right cursor** keys and the graph of $F_1(x) = 2x - 3$ with the trace option activated to display graph coordinates*

Note: In the rest of this appendix press **START**, press **RESET** and so on will be used to indicate that the appropriate black menu key is to be used for the word at the bottom of the screen.

Note also that **ENTER** and **OK** are alternative options and can be used as preferred when **OK** is present as a menu key. In the example above **OK** could have been used instead of **ENTER**.

GETTING STARTED WITH THE HP 38G

About the HP 38G

The HP 38G is made by Hewlett Packard Corporation and is available through your local calculator dealer. This appendix is not intended to be a product manual, but rather a convenient collection of "How to ..." descriptions of the procedures that are needed to complete all tasks within this book. Teachers are strongly advised to familiarize themselves with all the features of the graphics calculator in this appendix.

Managing a work session

How to turn the HP 38G on/off

● To turn the HP 38G on, press **ON** .

● To turn the HP 38G off, press ▢ which is blue and then **ON** . (Note that the function **OFF** is printed above the **ON** key in blue.)

Note: The HP 38G has an automatic "shutdown" feature which powers the HP 38G down after a few minutes. However, the contents of the display are saved for when it is next turned on. This means that any functions entered, graphs plotted and changes to the viewing window dimensions are still in the calculator's memory. It is important to be aware of this and wise to establish a routine of "clearing" any existing functions and returning to the default viewing window before starting on a new activity. "Resetting" the calculator involves deleting all data (including any programs) and restoring all default settings.

How to clear all existing information

Often you wish to begin a work session by clearing all previously entered information. To achieve this, perform the following steps.

Step 1   After turning the calculator on, press **LIB** (to access the **APLET LIBRARY**).

Step 2   Locate the **Function** aplet and press **RESET**, and then press **YES** (to confirm). This resets all the default options for this aplet, including a viewing window with dimensions $-6.5 \leq x \leq 6.5$ and $-3.1 \leq y \leq 3.2$. It also clears any function rule that may have been entered previously.

Entering and plotting functions

With the HP 38G, the rules for functions are entered via the calculator keys. A maximum of 10 functions may be entered concurrently. The notation used to define each function is the $F_n(x)$ format, where n is an integer between 1 to 10 inclusive.

How to enter and plot a function

Step 1   Press **LIB** and then highlight the **Function** aplet.

Step 2   Press **START** to enter the **Function** aplet (for working with function rules and graphs).

Note: These first two steps are not necessary each time you wish to enter and plot a function, but are essential procedures for beginning a work session in the **Function** aplet.

The screen shown below should appear. Note that the screen can fit five function rules. There are, in fact, 10 function definitions permitted, but the others are off screen and can be accessed with the **down cursor** key.

Step 3   Press the keys required to create a function rule. To represent the independent variable x, press the variable key **X,T,θ**. In this example, type in the function $F_1(x) = x^2 + 3x + 2$ by pressing the following sequence of keys.

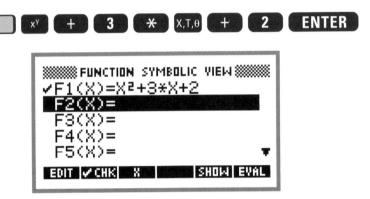

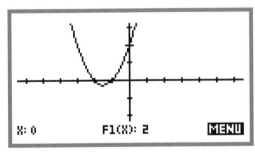

The function definition screen on the HP 38G

If you have made errors when entering the function (for example, wrong symbol), use the cursor keys to return to the location of the incorrect symbol, and press the correct keys. This should replace the old symbol with the new correct one.

Step 4   Press PLOT to view the graph of the function you have entered.

Note: The above procedure assumes that you are using the default viewing window. If your graph does not look like the one below, press ⬜ and then LIB (**VIEWS**). Move the cursor keys to highlight the **Decimal** view and then press OK. This creates a plot in the default window $-6.5 \leq x \leq 6.5$ and $-3.1 \leq y \leq 3.2$, with decimal (0.1) trace increments.

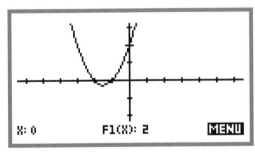

The graph of the function $F_1(x) = x^2 + 3x + 2$ plotted on the HP 38G

How to enter and plot more than one function

If you wish to enter and plot a number of functions on the same set of axes, follow these steps.

Step 1   Enter the first function as described in the section above entitled "How to enter and plot a function."

Step 2   To enter further functions, press SYMB to move to the function rule screen.

Step 3   Highlight the next empty function rule line.

Step 4   Type the appropriate keys to enter the desired functions.

Step 5   Repeat steps 3 and 4 until all functions have been entered.

Step 6   Press PLOT to display the graphs of all entered functions.

How to enter and plot a function using parameters

It is possible to change the rule and re-plot a function without editing a function directly. To do this it is possible to enter a function rule including parameters (constants). For example, we can enter a function of the form $f(x) = A(x-2)^2 + 1$, where A is the parameter. By assigning different values for A, we are able to change the function rule and its associated graph without re-entering the function rule.

Step 1   Press SYMB to move to the function rule screen.

Step 2   Clear any existing function rules and then press the required keys to complete entering the rule $f(x) = A(x-2)^2 + 1$. To enter A use A...Z HOME .

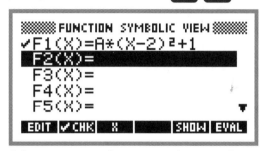

Function definition screen showing a rule using the parameter A

Step 3   Press ENTER to store the function.

Step 4   Press HOME to move to the **HOME** screen.

Step 5   Press the following keys to store 1.4 as the value of A.

Step 6   Press PLOT and then PLOT again to replot the graph of the function.

Step 7   Repeat steps 4, 5 and 6 to try other values of A as required.

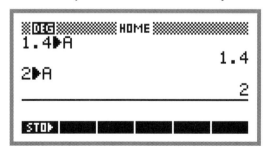

HOME screen showing two values for the parameter A

How to plot a family of functions

A family of functions is a set of functions that are identical except for the value of a particular constant. For example, $f(x) = x^2 - 2$, $f(x) = x^2$ and $f(x) = x^2 + 2$ are all member functions of a family, written as $f(x) = x^2 + a$. With a HP 38G, we can work with a family of functions by following the procedure below.

Note: The following procedure assumes that you are using the default viewing window.

In this example the function family will be of the form $F_1(x) = x^2 + a$, where $a = \{-2, 0, 2\}$.

Step 1   Press SYMB to move to the function rule screen.

Step 2   Clear any existing function rules and then press the required keys to enter the rules.
Press **ENTER** after each rule.

$$F1(X) = X^2 - 2$$
$$F2(X) = X^2$$
$$F2(X) = X^2 + 2$$

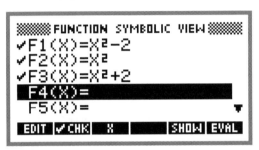

Defining examples from the function family $f(x) = x^2 + a$

Step 3   Press PLOT to plot the graphs of these functions.

This creates the three graphs $y = x^2 - 2$, $y = x^2$ and $y = x^2 + 2$.

The graph of $f(x) = x^2 + a$ will be plotted for $a = -2$, 0 and 2 (see resultant graphs below). The method of data entry shown in the above example is very useful for quickly observing the impact of a particular constant on the shape of a graph.

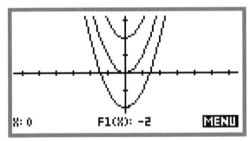

The family of functions of the form $f(x) = x^2 + a$ for $a = -2$, 0 and 2

Entering brackets, exponents and fractions

The syntax rules on the HP 38G strictly follow the normal rules for the order of mathematical operations (for example, brackets, exponents, division and multiplication, then addition and subtraction). A function rule, when defined, occupies a single line and therefore can be hard to read. For example, an expression such as:

$$F_2(x) = \frac{x - 3}{x + 2}$$

will appear on screen as **F2(X)=(X–3)/(X+2)**.

When entering function rules, pay careful attention to the order of operations. When in doubt, use brackets to make your intention clear.

How to enter brackets

Step 1   Press 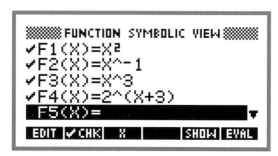 (to open the brackets.

Step 2   Enter any symbols/terms that should be within the brackets.

Step 3   Press) to close the brackets.

How to enter exponents (powers)

● If the exponent is 2 (that is, for x^2) press X,T,θ followed by [ ] and then x^y ($\mathbf{x^2}$).

● If the exponent is −1 (that is, for x^{-1}) press X,T,θ followed by [ ] and then X,T,θ ($\mathbf{x^{-1}}$).

● If the exponent is a number other than 2 or −1, (for example, x^3) press X,T,θ followed by x^y followed by the exponent (for example, 3).

● If the exponent is not a single term (for example, 2^{x+3}) make sure that you bracket the terms that are exponents (for example, **2^(X+3)**).

```
░░░░FUNCTION SYMBOLIC VIEW░░░░
✔F1(X)=X²
✔F2(X)=X^-1
✔F3(X)=X^3
✔F4(X)=2^(X+3)
 F5(X)=                        ▼
 EDIT ✔CHK   X        SHOW EVAL
```

Some examples of the syntax displayed when entering
exponents on a HP 38G

How to enter fractions

Step 1   For simple fractions, press the keys for the numerator.

Step 2   Press / (it will appear as / on the screen).

Step 3   Press the keys for the denominator.

Step 4   For more complicated fractions (involving more than one term in either the numerator or denominator or both), ensure that you use brackets to preserve the order of operations. Some examples are shown below.

```
░░░░FUNCTION SYMBOLIC VIEW░░░░
✔F1(X)=2/3
✔F2(X)=2*X/3
✔F3(X)=(2*X+3)/7
✔F4(X)=(2*X+3)/(X-1)
 F5(X)=                        ▼
 EDIT ✔CHK   X        SHOW EVAL
```

Some examples of the appropriate use of fractions and brackets
when entering function rules

127

Clearing function rules and graphs

How to clear a function rule and its graph

Note: The following procedure assumes you are already in the **Function** aplet.

Step 1   Press **SYMB** to bring the defined function rules into view.

Step 2   Use the cursor keys to move to the function rule you wish to clear.

Step 3   Press **DEL** to clear the rule.

Step 4   Repeat steps 2 and 3 to clear any other function rules and their graphs.

Note: It is possible to clear all function rules by pressing ▭ and **DEL** (**CLEAR**).

See also "How to stop the HP 38G from plotting a graph" in the next section.

WORKING WITH FUNCTION GRAPHS ON THE HP 38G

Working with the graph window

How to display graph coordinates

Note: The following procedure assumes you are in the **Function** aplet, and have entered a suitable function as $F_1(x)$.

Step 1   Press **PLOT** to plot the graph of the function.

Step 2   Press the right cursor key. This locates the cursor on the graph of the function $F_1(x)$, allowing the user to trace the function along the path of $F_1(x)$. The coordinates of the function that is currently being traced are being displayed (see diagram below).

Step 3   Use the **left** and **right cursor** keys to trace the path of the function. The coordinates of the cursor are updated each time the cursor keys are pressed.

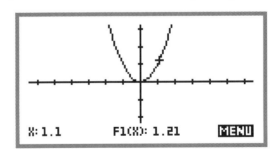

The graph of $F_1(x) = x^2$ with the trace option activated to display graph coordinates

Step 4   If you wish to trace the function $F_2(x)$, $F_3(x)$ or another function graph that you have defined, press the **down cursor** key to move the cursor to the other function graphs. The number of the function will be displayed in the bottom center of the screen (see example below) indicating which function graph coordinates are currently being displayed.

Use the **left** and **right cursor** keys to trace the path of the function. The coordinates of the cursor are updated each time the cursor keys are pressed.

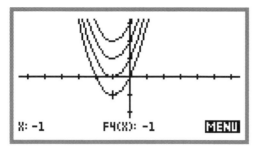

*Using the trace option and the **down cursor** keys to display the coordinates of $F_4(x)$*

Note: If the trace option is not working, press MENU and then TRACE to turn the trace option on. Press MENU and then TRACE to turn off.

How to stop the HP 38G from plotting a graph

Each time a new function is defined in the **F(X)=** screen, the HP 38G assumes you will want to graph it, so if you press PLOT, the calculator will attempt to plot the new function. If you wish to prevent the HP 38G from plotting any function, follow the next procedure.

Note: The following procedure assumes you are already in the **Function** aplet with a function entered in F1X.

Step 1   Press SYMB to bring the defined function rules into view.

Step 2   Use the cursor keys to highlight the function rule F1(X).

Step 3   Press CHK to prevent this function from being plotted.

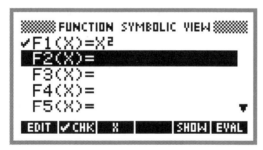

Function $F_1(x)$ checked, to be plotted

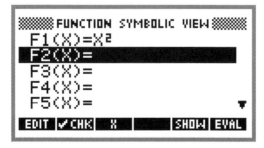

Function $F_1(x)$ unchecked, not to be plotted

Step 4   To re-plot an unchecked function, repeat the process to check the function again.

129

How to display the function rule and graph simultaneously

Once the function has been plotted, it is possible to display its associated rule by following these steps.

Step 1   Press **MENU** (this step assumes that you have already plotted a function rule).

Step 2   Press **DEFN** This locates the cursor on the graph of the function $F_1(x)$, with the associated function rule displayed in the bottom left of the screen.

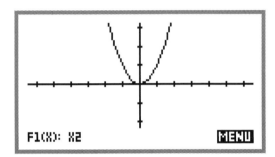

Using the **MENU DEFN** *feature to view both the function rule and its graph simultaneously*

Changing the viewing window

The graph screen can be thought of as a true "window" through which we can observe the graphs of defined functions. If the relevant portion(s) of the function's graph are not quite in view, there are a number of options for changing the viewing window so that we can more clearly examine the behavior of the function.

How to change to the default viewing window

Press [   ] and then **LIB** (VIEWS). Move the cursor to highlight **Decimal** and then press **OK**. This creates a plot in the default window $-6.5 \leq x \leq 6.5$ and $-3.1 \leq y \leq 3.2$, with decimal (0.1) trace increments.

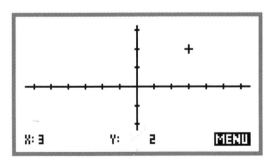

The default viewing window for the HP 38G is $-6.5 \leq x \leq 6.5$ *and* $-3.1 \leq y \leq 3.2$

How to specify the viewing window dimensions

Step 1   Press [   ], then **PLOT**. This will bring up the **FUNCTION PLOT SETUP** as shown below (assuming you are in the **Function** aplet).

*Changing the viewing window by using the **PLOT** key*

Step 2   Use the cursor keys to move to the option you wish to alter. Then enter the new figure, pressing **ENTER** after each value. The available options are explained below.

XRNG—the minimum/maximum x value that will be visible in the viewing window.

YRNG—the minimum/maximum y value that will be visible in the viewing window.

XTICK—the number of units between markings on the x-axis.

YTICK—the number of units between markings on the y-axis.

Step 3   Press **PLOT** to show the resultant change in the viewing window.

How to locate a graph not visible in the current viewing window

Sometimes the graph may not be displayed in the current viewing window. The HP 38G has a feature which adjusts the **YRNG** values so that the graph of the function comes into view (for the current x values).

Step 1   Press the required keys to enter the rule $F_1(x) = x^2 + 12$.

Step 2   Press [ ] and then **LIB** (VIEWS).

Step 3   Move the cursor to the **Decimal** view and then press **OK**. This creates a plot in the default window $-6.5 \le x \le 6.5$ and $-3.1 \le y \le 3.2$, with decimal (0.1) trace increments. Note that the graph is not in view.

Step 4   Press [ ] and then **LIB** (VIEWS).

Step 5   Move the cursor to the **Auto Scale** view and then press **OK** to "locate" the graph for the current x values. This adjusts the **YRNG** values so that the graph comes into view.

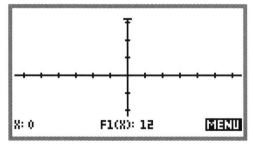
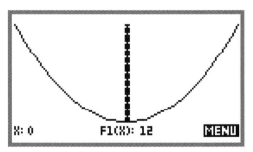

*Using the **VIEWS** **Auto Scale** feature to create a better view (right diagram) of the graph than the view possible in the default viewing window (left diagram)*

How to change the center of the viewing window

The cursor keys allow the user to make adjustments to the viewing window so that a relevant part of the graph may come into view. This is done by invoking a zoom command which will render the current location of the trace cursor as the center of the new viewing window.

Step 1   Press the required keys to enter the rule $F_1(x) = x^2 - 4$.

Step 2   Press ⬛ and then **LIB** (VIEWS).

Step 3   Move the cursor to the **Decimal** view and then press **OK**. This creates a plot in the default window $-6.5 \leq x \leq 6.5$ and $-3.1 \leq y \leq 3.2$, with decimal (0.1) trace increments.

Note: The vertex or turning point of the parabola is not in view, and the cursor appears to be located at the point $(0, -4)$. The following steps will re-center the viewing window around this point.

Step 4   Press **MENU** and then **ZOOM**. This will bring up the zoom options.

Step 5   Locate the **Center** zoom option and press **OK**. This will redraw the function in a viewing window with the point $(0, -4)$ at its center.

Using scaling/zooming options

Scaling is the process of changing the scales on either or both axes. Graphing calculators often refer to the process of zooming in and zooming out:

● **zooming in**—looking more closely at the graph through a smaller viewing window;

● **zooming out**—looking more widely at the graph through a larger viewing window.

Zooming in permits the user to focus more precisely on a portion of the graph. With the HP 38G, there are three main ways to zoom in:

● Use the **FUNCTION PLOT SETUP** to make the viewing window include a smaller region of the X–Y plane (see "How to specify the viewing window dimensions").

● Use **ZOOM** and the **In** option to select a new viewing window center point and zoom in around that point.

● Use **ZOOM** and the **Box...** option to select and zoom in to a "boxed" region within the current viewing window.

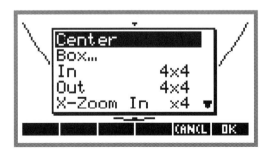 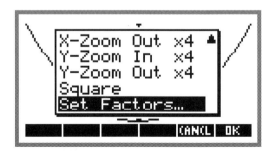

The options available after pressing MENU ZOOM from the graph window

How to return to the default zoom level

Step 1   Press ▢ and then **LIB** (VIEWS). (Assumes you are in the **Function** aplet.)

Step 2   Move the cursor to the **Decimal** view and then press **OK**. This creates a plot in the default window $-6.5 \leq x \leq 6.5$ and $-3.1 \leq y \leq 3.2$, with decimal (0.1) trace increments.

How to zoom in with the In option

The **In** option permits zooming in, based on the current viewing window. The HP 38G defaults to zooming in on both axes by a factor of four.

Step 1   Press the required keys to enter the rule $F_1(x) = x^2$.

Step 2   Press ▢ and then **LIB** (VIEWS).

Step 3   Move the cursor to the **Decimal** view and then press **OK**. This creates a plot in the default window $-6.5 \leq x \leq 6.5$ and $-3.1 \leq y \leq 3.2$, with decimal (0.1) trace increments.

Step 4   Press the **right** (or **left**) **cursor** key to locate the cursor on the graph in the area of interest.

Step 5   Press **MENU** and then **ZOOM** to bring up the zoom options.

Step 6   Move the cursor to **In** and then press **OK** to zoom in by a factor of four around the current location of the Trace cursor.

Step 7   To zoom in further, press **MENU** and **ZOOM**, select **In** again and press **OK**.

Note: Each use of **ZOOM In** divides the value of both the **XRNG** and **YRNG** by four.

How to box zoom with the Box... option

The **ZOOM Box** option permits zooming inside a user definable rectangular "box" of the current viewing window. This box becomes the new viewing window.

Step 1   Press the required keys to enter the rule $F_1(x) = x^2$.

Step 2   Press ▢ and then **LIB** (VIEWS).

Step 3   Move the cursor to the **Decimal** view and then press **OK**. This creates a plot in the default window $-6.5 \leq x \leq 6.5$ and $-3.1 \leq y \leq 3.2$, with decimal (0.1) trace increments.

Step 4   Press **MENU** and then **ZOOM** to bring up the zoom options.

Step 5   Move the cursor to **Box ...** and then press **OK**.

Step 6   Use the cursor keys to locate the upper left corner of the zoom box.

Step 7   Press **OK**.

Step 8   Use the cursor keys to locate the bottom right corner of the zoom box (a box will be created on screen).

Step 9   Press **OK**. (This now zooms into the boxed region.)

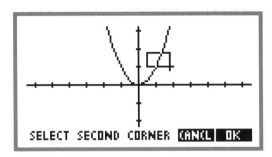

*Zooming in using the **Box...** option. Note the box that has been defined*

How to zoom out with the Out option

Zooming out permits the user to observe more of the graph, including perhaps more of the general shape or global features of the graph. The HP 38G defaults to zooming out on both axes by a factor of four.

Step 1   Press the required keys to enter the rule $F_1(x) = x^2$.

Step 2   Press [ ] and then **LIB** (VIEWS).

Step 3   Move the cursor to the **Decimal** view and then press **OK**. This creates a plot in the default window $-6.5 \le x \le 6.5$ and $-3.1 \le y \le 3.2$, with decimal (0.1) trace increments.

Step 4   Press the **right** (or **left**) **cursor** key to locate the cursor on the graph in the area of interest.

Step 5   Press **MENU** and then **ZOOM** to bring up the zoom options.

Step 6   Move the cursor to **Out** and then press **OK** to zoom out by a factor of four around the current location of the trace cursor.

Step 7   To zoom out further, press **MENU** and **ZOOM**, select **Out** again and press **OK**.

Note: Each use of **ZOOM** **Out** quadruples the value of both the XRNG and YRNG by four.

How to use the Integer option

The **Integer** option on the VIEWS screen permits the user to trace functions by redefining the viewing window so that each press of the trace cursor increments x by 1 unit. This may be useful if you are considering integer only solutions to problems. This may also be useful if you are wishing to trace a function, incrementing by integer values of the independent variable, rather than incrementing by amounts dependent on the current zoom level.

Step 1   Press the required keys to enter the rule $F_1(x) = x^2$.

Step 2   Press [ ] and then **LIB** (VIEWS).

Step 3   Move the cursor to the **Decimal** view and then press **OK**. This creates a plot in the default window $-6.5 \le x \le 6.5$ and $-3.1 \le y \le 3.2$, with decimal (0.1) trace increments.

Step 4   Press [ ] and then **LIB** (VIEWS) to access the VIEWS options.

Step 5   Move the cursor to **Integer** and press **OK**. This creates a plot in the default window $-65 \le x \le 65$ and $-3.1 \le y \le 3.2$, with integer trace increments.

Step 6   Press the **right cursor** key to calculate the function value for successive integer values of the independent variable.

How to use the Square option

The ▨ZOOM▨ **Square** option attempts to display the true graph proportions by replotting the graphs of all entered functions with equal scales for the x- and y-axes. It does this by altering the current viewing window so that pressing the **left** or **right cursor** key moves the cursor the same distance as pressing the up or down cursor key.

Step 1   Press the required keys to enter the rule $F_1(x) = x$.

Step 2   Press ▭ and then ▨PLOT▨ to edit the viewing window dimensions.

Step 3   Change **XRNG** to $-10 \leq x \leq 10$ and **YRNG** to $-10 \leq y \leq 10$, and then press ▨PLOT▨.

Note: The linear graph should be at 45° with respect to the x-axis, but is not. Note also how the axis markings on the y-axis are differently spaced to those on the x-axis.

Step 1   Press ▨MENU▨ and then ▨ZOOM▨ to bring up the zoom options.

Step 2   Highlight **Square** using the cursor keys and then press ▨ OK ▨.

This plots the function in a viewing window in which true proportions are displayed. (It will also create axis markings that have equivalent spacing on each axis.)

How to change the zoom factors

The default zoom factor is four for each axis. This means that zooming in (or out) creates a change in the magnification of 400% in the direction of each axis. The procedure for changing any or all of these zoom factors is given below.

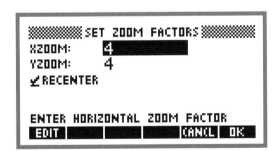

*The **Set Factors** ... option (for changing the zoom factors)*

Step 1   Press ▨MENU▨ and then ▨ZOOM▨ to bring up the zoom options.

Step 2   Move the cursor to **Set Factors ...** and then press ▨ OK ▨.

Step 3   Change the values of **XZOOM** or **YZOOM** as required.

Step 4   Press ▨ OK ▨ to return to the graph screen.

WORKING WITH ADDITIONAL FEATURES ON THE HP 38G

Creating a table of function values

Creating a table of values from the function allows the user to observe another representation of the function. It could be a more convenient way of listing the function values of a number of functions at once.

The example given below is to create a table of values for the function $f(x) = x^2$ with increments of 0.1.

How to create a table of values

Step 1   Press the required keys to enter the rule $F_1(x) = x^2$.

Step 2   Press ⬜ and then NUM to enter table parameters on the function numeric setup screen.

Step 3   Enter 23 as **NUMSTART** (minimum x value for table).

Step 4   Enter 0.1 as **NUMSTEP** (increment for x values in table).

Setting the table options

Step 5   Press NUM to view the table of function values. The result is shown below.

Step 6   Use the cursor keys to scroll down the list.

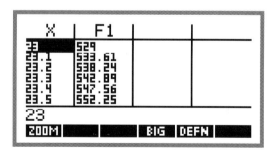

Sample table for $f(x) = x^2$ for increments in the x values of 0.1

136

Plotting points

When attempting to fit functions to data that has been collected, it is convenient to plot data points, and then attempt to find function graphs which seem to line up with the points. The sample chart below illustrates a possible scenario where plotting points might be used.

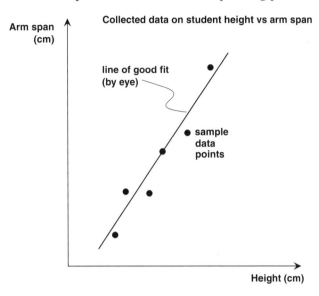

How to change the display precision

When entering data, it is useful to set the display precision first so that the data is displayed with the appropriate number of decimal points.

Step 1   Press ⬜ and then **HOME** (**MODES**) to set up the display precision.

Step 2   Move the cursor to **NUMBER FORMAT ...** and then press **CHOOS**.

Step 3   Use the **down cursor** key to select either a fixed display precision (**Fixed**) of 0–9 decimal points, or floating precision (**Standard**) to allow the HP 38G to select the display precision dependent on the figures entered and calculations performed.

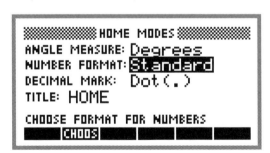

Using the MODES screen to change the display precision

How to plot points

In this example, use the following data values.

x	1	2	3	4	5	6
y	2.2	3.5	4.7	6.6	7.2	9.1

Step 1   **LIB** (to access the aplet library).

Step 2   Locate the **Statistics** aplet and press **RESET**, and then press **YES** (to confirm).
          This resets all the default options for this aplet, deleting any existing data and plots.

Step 3   Press **START** to launch the statistics aplet.

Step 4   Enter the *x* values above into the column **C1**. Press **OK** after each entry.

Step 5   Enter the *y* values above into the column **C2**. Press **OK** after each entry.

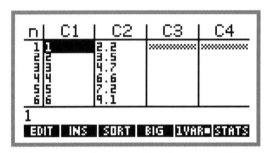

*Table of values for x and y shown in the data lists of the **Statistics** aplet*

Step 6   Press **1VAR** to toggle to **2VAR**. This means that we will be treating **C1** and **C2** as a
          bivariate data set.

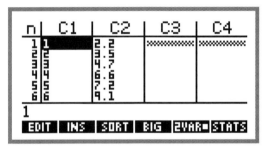

*The same screen as above, but with **2VAR** selected as the preferred analysis*

Step 7   Press ▢ and then **PLOT** to indicate that you wish to set up a plot. A screen will
          appear displaying the plot options, such as the viewing window dimensions and the
          marker to be used for plotting. We will accept the default options.

Setting statistical plot options for S1

Step 8   Press ▢ and then **LIB** (VIEWS) to access the **VIEWS** options.

Step 9 Locate the **Auto Scale** option and press 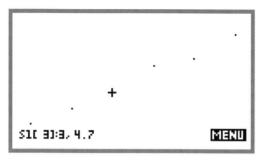 OK . This will plot the data points for **S1**(Statistical Graph 1) in an appropriate viewing window.

Step 10 Using the **right** and **left cursor** keys allows you to observe the coordinates of each point.

*A scatter plot of the above data plotted in the **Statistics** aplet*

How to fit a function to data by eye

It is possible to try different functions that might fit the data points. One useful way of constructing such functions on the HP 38G is to use the fit function.

In this example (using the data entered and plotted above), we will try to fit a function of the form $y = Ax$, where A is the parameter that we will alter to try to achieve a good fit.

Note: This procedure assumes that you have completed the procedure above, entitled "How to plot points" and have not reset the **Statistics** aplet.

Step 1 Press ▭ and then SYMB to set up the fit parameters in the STATISTICS SYMBOLIC SETUP window.

Step 2 Locate the cursor on the S1FIT line and press CHOOS. This will bring up the fit options.

Step 3 Locate the **User Defined** fit option and press OK .

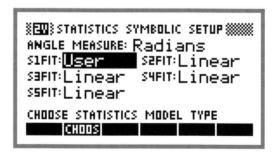

The STATISTICS SYMBOLIC SETUP window with the S1FIT line selected

Step 4 Press SYMB and move to the **Fit1** line.

Step 5 Enter the rule for the fit as 1.4x and then press OK . To enter the "x", press the "x" symbol at the bottom of the screen, rather than the X,T,θ key.

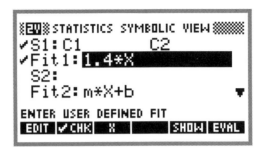

*The **SYMB** screen after parameter A has been set to 1.4x in **Fit1***

Step 6 Press **PLOT** to return to the screen which displays the scatter plot.

Step 7 Press **MENU** and then press **FIT** (to toggle to **FIT ◻**) to observe whether the graph of $F_1(x) = 1.4x$ has given a good fit for the data set present.

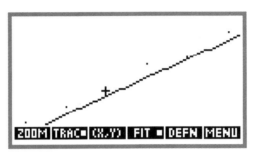

*The graph screen after the **User Defined** fit rule $F_1(x) = 1.4x$
overlays the scatter plot*

To try other values of *A*:

Step 1 Press **SYMB** and edit the **User Defined** fit rule for **Fit1**.

Step 2 Press **OK** to update this rule.

Step 3 Press **PLOT** to return to the screen which displays the scatter plot, and the new **FIT**.

Note: To clear any drawn graphs, press **MENU** and then **FIT ◻**.

Appendix D
Working with the TI-82/83

TI-82/83 QUICK START!

This "Quick Start" page describes the four steps necessary to enter and plot a function with the TI-82/83, using the example function $f(x) = 2x - 3$. A more detailed set of instructions for entering and plotting functions can be found in the next section of this appendix.

Four "Quick Start" steps to enter and plot a function

Step 1   To turn the TI-82/83 on, press **ON** at the bottom left of the calculator keys.

Step 2   Press **Y=** . Press the keys required to create a function rule. To represent the independent variable X, the TI-82/83 uses the variable key **X,T,θ**. In this example, type in the function $Y_1 = 2x - 3$ by pressing the following sequence of keys;

Step 3   Press **ZOOM**, then press **6** (6 : ZStandard). This creates a plot of the function in the "standard" viewing window which is $-10 \le x \le 10$ and $-10 \le y \le 10$.

Step 4   Press **TRACE**. This locates the cursor on the graph of the function Y_1, allowing the user to trace the function along the path of Y_1. The symbol **1** is displayed in the top right-hand corner of the screen to indicate that Y_1 is the function whose coordinates are being displayed (see diagram below). Use the **left** and **right cursor** keys to "trace" the path of the function. The coordinates of the cursor are updated each time the cursor keys are pressed.

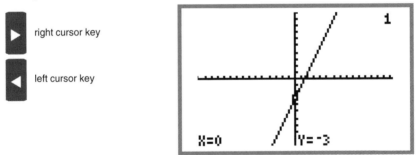

right cursor key

left cursor key

*The left and right cursor keys and the graph of $Y_1 = 2x - 3$ with the **Trace** option activated to display graph coordinates*

Note: On the TI-83, the function rule is displayed in the top left of the screen when the **TRACE** feature is on.

GETTING STARTED WITH THE TI-82/83

About the TI-82/83

The TI-82 and TI-83 are made by Texas Instruments and are available through your local calculator dealer. This appendix is not intended to be a product manual, but rather a convenient collection of "How to …" descriptions of the procedures that are needed to complete all tasks within this book. Teachers are strongly advised to familiarize themselves with all the features of the graphic calculator in this appendix.

142

Please note: This appendix is designed for both the TI-82 and TI-83, whose basic functions operate in a very similar way. All screen dumps are taken from a TI-82, and comments have been inserted in the text where the procedure on a TI-83 differs from that on a TI-82.

Managing a work session

How to turn the TI-82/83 on/off

- To turn the TI-82/83 on, press ON at the bottom left of the calculator keys.

- To turn the TI-82/83 off, press 2nd and then ON . (Note that the second function **OFF** is printed above the key on the left.)

Note: The TI-82/83 has an automatic "shutdown" feature which powers the TI-82/83 down after a few minutes. However, the contents of the display are saved for when it is next turned on. This means that any functions entered, graphs plotted and changes to the viewing window dimensions are still in the calculator's memory. It is important to be aware of this and wise to establish a routine of "clearing" any existing functions and returning to the default viewing window before starting on a new activity.

After turning on the TI-82/83, the screen that appears is the home screen. It may or may not be empty, depending on what calculations had been entered prior to when the calculator was last powered down. Since other items are still in memory, such as previously defined functions and the viewing window dimensions, it is wise to begin a work session by clearing such information.

How to clear all existing information

Step 1 After turning the calculator on, press CLEAR . This should clear the home screen.

Step 2 Press GRAPH .

- If it is not blank, press Y= . If there are function rules, move the cursor keys to each non-blank line and then press CLEAR to remove any existing graphs.
- If the graph screen is blank (except for the axes), move to the next step.

Step 3 Press 2nd and then **QUIT** to return to the home screen.

Step 4 Press ZOOM and then select the **6 : ZStandard** option to return to the standard viewing window.

Step 5 Press 2nd and then **STAT PLOT**. Press **4 : Plots off** to clear any statistical plots.

After completing these steps, you will be ready to commence a work session with the TI-82/83. *Note:* A quicker way to clear all information is to:

TI-82
- press 2nd and then **MEM**;
- press **3 : Reset** and then **2 : Reset** (to confirm). This will clear all data (including any programs) and restore all default settings.

TI-83
- press 2nd and then **MEM**;
- press **5 : Reset** and then **2 : Defaults**. This will restore all default settings (without destroying any stored data or programs).

Special note: If the battery is low, "resetting" the TI-82/83 may cause the display to disappear. Press 2nd and hold down the up cursor key to improve screen contrast.

Entering and plotting functions

With the TI-82/83, the rules for functions are entered via the calculator keys. A maximum of 10 functions may be entered concurrently. The notation used to define each function is the Y_n format, where n is an integer between 1 to 10 inclusive.

How to enter and plot a function

Step 1 Press Y= . The screen below should appear. Note that the screen can fit eight function definitions. There are, in fact, ten function definitions permitted, but two (Y_9 and Y_{10}) are off screen and can be accessed with the down cursor key.

Step 2 Press the keys required to create a function rule. To represent the independent variable X, press the variable key **X,T,θ**. In this example, type in the function $Y_1 = x^2 + 3x + 2$ by pressing the following sequence of keys:

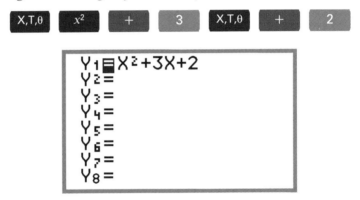

The Function definition screen on the TI-82/83

Step 3 If you have made errors when entering the function (for example, wrong symbol), use the cursor keys to return to the location of the incorrect symbol, and press the correct keys. This should replace the old symbol with the new correct one.

Step 4 Press ZOOM and then 6 to select the **6 : ZStandard** option to return to the standard viewing window.

Step 5 When the function is complete, press GRAPH and the graph shown below will appear on the screen.

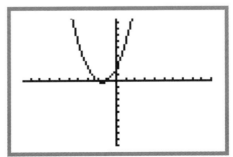

The graph of the function $Y_1 = x^2 + 3x + 2$ plotted on the TI-82/83

How to enter and plot more than one function

If you wish to enter and plot several functions, all on the same set of axes, follow the steps given below.

Step 1   Enter the first function as described in "How to enter and plot a function."

Step 2   To enter further functions, press  Y= and move the cursor to the next empty function rule line.

Step 3   Type the appropriate keys to enter the desired functions.

Step 4   Repeat steps 2 and 3 until all functions have been entered.

Step 5   Press GRAPH to display the graphs of all entered functions.

How to enter and plot a function using parameters

It is possible to change the rule and re-plot a function without using Y= . To do this it is possible to enter a function rule including parameters (constants). For example, we can enter a function of the form $y = Ax$, where A is the parameter. By assigning different values for A, we can change the function rule and its associated graph without re-entering the function rule.

Step 1   Press Y= .

Step 2   To enter the parameter A, press ALPHA, followed by MATH which has the alpha function **A** printed above the key on the right.

Step 3   Press the required keys to complete entering the rule $Y_1 = A(X - 2)^2 + 1$.

The Function definition screen showing a rule using the parameter A

Step 4   Press 2nd and then **QUIT** to return to the Home screen.

Step 5   To enter a specific value for A in the Home screen (for example, $A = 1.4$), press the following key sequence:

1 . 4 STO ALPHA MATH ENTER

This sets the current value of the parameter **A** to 1.4.

Step 6   Press GRAPH to observe the graph.

Step 7   Try other values of A as required by repeating steps 5 and 6. The Home screen will look something like the one on the following page.

```
1.4→A
                    1.4
2→A
                     2
1.7→A
                    1.7
```

Home screen after entering three different values for the parameter A

How to plot a family of functions

A family of functions is a set of functions that are identical except for the value of a particular constant. For example, $f(x) = x^2 - 1$, $f(x) = x^2 + 2$ and $f(x) = x^2 + 3.25$ are all member functions of a family, written as $f(x) = x^2 + a$. With a TI-82/83, we can work with a family of functions by following the procedure below.

In this example the function family will be of the form $Y_1 = x^2 + a$, where $a = \{-2, 0, 2\}$.

Step 1   Press [Y=] to define a function.

Step 2   Enter the rule for the function, by entering the following sequence:

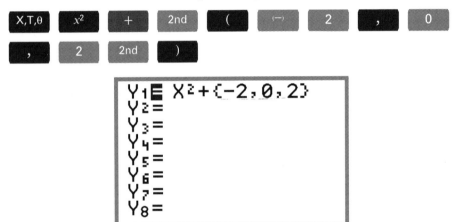

```
Y₁■ X²+{-2,0,2}
Y₂=
Y₃=
Y₄=
Y₅=
Y₆=
Y₇=
Y₈=
```

Defining a function with changeable constants.
This creates the three graphs $y = x^2 - 2$, $y = x^2$ and $y = x^2 + 2$

The graph of $f(x) = x^2 + a$ will be plotted for $a = -2$, 0, and 2 (see resultant graphs below). The method of data entry shown in the above example is very useful for quickly observing the impact of a particular constant on the shape of a graph.

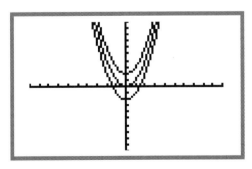

The family of functions of the form $f(x) = x^2 + a$ for $a = -2$, 0 and 2

How to restrict the domain of a function

The set of defined x values for which the function is defined is called the "domain" of the function. Let us say, for example, that a function $f(x) = x^2$ is only defined for $-3 \leq x \leq 2.5$. It is possible for the TI-82/83 to incorporate this restriction by following the procedure listed below.

Step 1 Press MODE .

Step 2 Position the cursor on the line that contains the **Connected/Dot** option.

Step 3 Select the **Dot** option and press ENTER . (This is the only mode in which functions with restricted domains will work properly.)

Step 4 Press Y= and press the appropriate keys to enter the function:
$$Y_1 = (x^2)\,(x \geq -3)\,(x \leq 2.5)$$

Note: Keys such as $\leq$ and $\geq$ are entered by pressing 2nd and then TEST and the appropriate number.

Defining the function $y = x^2$ with a restricted domain of $-3 \leq x \leq 2.5$

This bracketing of statements within the rule and domain (see the function in the illustration above) looks a little cumbersome, and working in **Dot** mode does not usually give the best view of a function, but domain restrictions and hybrid or piece-wise functions are quite possible on TI-82/83.

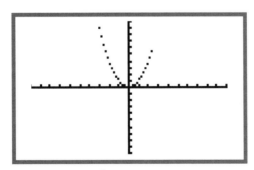

The graph of the function $y = x^2$ with a restricted domain of $-3 \leq x \leq 2.5$

After pressing GRAPH , the graph of $f(x)$ should now appear, incorporating the restricted values for x. Note how the function is only plotted between $x = -3$ and $x = 2.5$. This procedure of restricting the function is very useful in modeling as it allows us to focus on the x values (domain) for which a rule makes sense.

Entering brackets, exponents and fractions

The syntax rules on the TI-82/83 strictly follow the normal rules for the order of mathematical operations (for example, brackets, exponents, division and multiplication, then addition and subtraction). A function rule, when defined, occupies a single line and therefore can be hard to read. For example, an expression such as:

$$Y_2 = \frac{x-3}{x+2}$$

will appear on screen as $Y_2 = (X - 3)/(X + 2)$.

When entering function rules, pay careful attention to the order of operations. When in doubt, use brackets to make your intention clear.

How to enter brackets

Step 1   Press (to open the brackets.

Step 2   Enter any symbols/terms that should be within the brackets.

Step 3   Press) to close the brackets.

How to enter exponents (powers)

- If the exponent is 2 (that is, for x^2) press X,T,θ followed by x^2 .

- If the exponent is −1 (that is, for x^{-1}) press X,T,θ followed by x^{-1} .

- If the exponent is a number other than 2 or ⁻1, (for example, x^3) press X,T,θ followed by ⌃ followed by the exponent (for example, 3).

- If the exponent is not a single term (for example, 2^{x+3}) make sure that you bracket the terms that are exponents (for example, 2^(x + 3).

```
Y₁🔲 X²
Y₂🔲 X⁻1
Y₃🔲 X^3
Y₄🔲 2^(X+3)█
Y₅ =
Y₆ =
Y₇ =
Y₈ =
```

Some examples of the syntax displayed when entering exponents on a TI-82/83

How to enter fractions

Step 1   For simple fractions, press the keys for the numerator.

Step 2   Press ÷ (it will appear as / on the screen).

Step 3   Press the keys for the denominator.

For more complicated fractions (involving more than one term in either the numerator or denominator or both), ensure that you use brackets to preserve the order of operations. Some examples are shown on the next page.

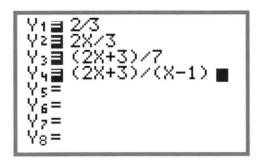

Some examples of the appropriate use of fractions and brackets when entering function rules

Clearing function rules and graphs

How to clear a function rule and its graph

Step 1   Press **Y=** . This will bring all defined function rules into view.

Step 2   Use the cursor keys to move to the function rule you wish to clear.

Step 3   Press **CLEAR** .

Step 4   Repeat steps 2 and 3 to clear any other function rules and their graphs.

See also "How to stop the TI-82/83 from plotting a graph" in the next section.

WORKING WITH FUNCTION GRAPHS ON THE TI-82/83

Working with the graph window

How to display graph coordinates

Step 1   Press **GRAPH** (this step assumes that you have already entered a function rule).

Step 2   Press **TRACE** . This locates the cursor on the graph of the function Y_1, allowing the user to trace the function along the path of Y_1. The symbol **1** is displayed in the top right hand corner of the screen to indicate that Y_1 is the function whose coordinates are being displayed (see diagram below).

Step 3   Use the **left and right cursor** keys to "trace" the path of the function. The coordinates of the cursor are updated each time the cursor keys are pressed.

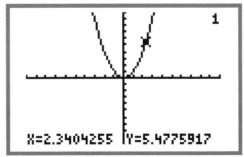

*The graph of $Y_1 = x^2$ with the **Trace** option activated to display graph coordinates*

149

Step 4   If you wish to trace the function Y_2, Y_3 or another function graph that you have defined, press the **down cursor** key to move the cursor to the other function graphs. The number displayed in the top right-hand corner of the screen (for example, 2 for Y_2, 3 for Y_3, and so on) indicates which function graph coordinates are currently being displayed.

Step 5   *Note:* On the TI-83, the function rule is displayed in the top left of the screen when the **TRACE** feature is on. This can be turned **Off/On** by pressing 2nd and then ZOOM for **FORMAT** and changing the **ExpON/ExpOFF** option.

Step 6   Use the **left** and **right cursor** keys to "trace" the path of the function. The coordinates of the cursor are updated each time the cursor keys are pressed.

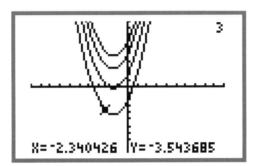

*Using the **Trace** and cursor keys to display the coordinates of Y_3*

How to stop the TI-82/83 from plotting a graph

Each time a new function is defined in the **Y=** screen, the TI-82/83 assumes you will want to graph it, so if you press GRAPH, the calculator will attempt to plot the new function. If you wish to prevent the TI-82/83 from plotting any function, follow the next procedure.

Step 1   Press Y= to bring up the Function definition screen. Note that the = symbol for Y_1 is blackened. This means that this function is "selected", and will be plotted.

Step 2   Press the **left cursor** key until the flashing cursor is on top of the = symbol for the function Y_1.

Step 3   Press ENTER. This de-selects the function, and removes the blackened background. It will now not plot the function Y_1. Confirm that this disables graphing the current function by pressing GRAPH.

Function Y_1 "selected"—to be plotted   *Function Y_1 "de-selected"—not to be plotted*

To re-plot a defined function, just repeat the above process to select the function Y_1 again. That is, move the cursor above the = symbol and press the ENTER key.

How to display the function rule and graph simultaneously

The TI-82/83 has a split-screen mode which allows you to view the **Graph** screen and one of the editing screens simultaneously. Thus you can observe the rule and the graph at the same time. To do this, follow these steps.

Note: The TI-83 will display the rule on the graph screen, and so this procedure may not be necessary.

Step 1   Press MODE.

Step 2   Press the **down cursor** key until it flashes over the **FullScreen/Split** mode line (or the **Full Horiz G-T** line on the TI-83).

Step 3   Press the **right cursor** key so that the cursor flashes over the **Split** option (or **Horiz** on the TI-83).

Step 4   Press ENTER to invoke this option.

Step 5   Press GRAPH to display the graph in the top half of the screen.

Step 6   Press Y= . Note that any defined function rule is displayed in the bottom half of the screen.

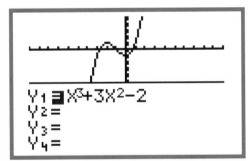

Using the split-screen mode to view both the function rule and its graph simultaneously

Changing the viewing window

The **Graph** screen can be thought of as a true "window" through which we can observe the graphs of defined functions. If the relevant portion(s) of the function graph are not quite in view, there are a number of options for changing the viewing window so that we can more clearly examine the behavior of the function.

How to change to the default viewing window

Step 1   Press ZOOM.

Step 2   Select the **6 : ZStandard** option and press ENTER. This will return to the default viewing window (the region bounded by the points $-10 \le x \le 10$ and $-10 \le y \le 10$).

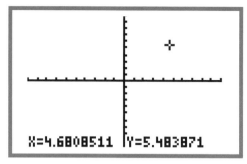

The default viewing window for the TI-82/83 ($-10 \leq x \leq 10$ and $-10 \leq y \leq 10$)

How to specify the viewing window dimensions

Step 1   Press WINDOW. This will bring up the screen shown below.

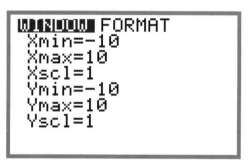

*Changing the viewing window by using the **Window** key*

Step 2   Use the **up** and **down cursor** keys to move to the **Window** option you wish to alter. Then enter the new figure. The available options are explained below.

Xmin/Xmax—the minimum/maximum x value that will be visible in the viewing window

Ymin/Ymax—the minimum/maximum y value that will be visible in the viewing window

Xscl/Yscl—the number of units between markings on the x-axis/y-axis

Note: The TI-83 also includes the option **Xres**, which is the pixel resolution (from 1 to 8). **Xres = 1** means one calculation per pixel and **Xres = 8** means one calculation every 8 pixels.

Step 3   Press GRAPH to show the resultant change in the viewing window.

How to locate a graph not visible in the current viewing window

Sometimes the graph may not be displayed in the current viewing window. The **Trace** key allows the user to locate the cursor on such a graph and to change the viewing window so that part of the graph will come into view.

Step 1   Press GRAPH to display the Graph screen (for this example, try $Y_1 = x^2 + 12$).

Step 2   Press TRACE to display graph coordinates. This locates the cursor on the graph of Y_1 (not on screen).

Step 3   If Y_1 is the graph that is not in view, press ENTER . This will reposition the viewing window so that a portion of the graph of Y_1 is now displayed (see example below for the graph of $y = x^2 + 12$.

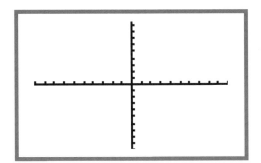 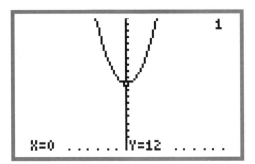

*Using the **Trace** feature to relocate the current viewing window (left diagram) to one that shows the graph (right diagram)*

If there is more than one function defined, and the function of interest is not Y_1, press the **down cursor** key (as required) to select the relevant graph. The upper right corner of the graph screen indicates which of the function graphs the cursor is located on (that is, 1 is displayed for Y_1, 2 for Y_2, and so on).

Then press ENTER to re-center the viewing window around the selected point.

Note: On the TI-83, the function rule is displayed in the top left of the screen when the TRACE feature is on.

How to change the center of the viewing window

Step 1   Press GRAPH to display the Graph screen.

Step 2   Press TRACE to display graph coordinates. This locates the cursor on the graph of Y_1, the first function defined.

Step 3   If Y_1 is the graph of interest, go to step 4. If there is more than one function defined, or if the function of interest is not Y_1, press the **up cursor** key (as required) to select the relevant graph. The upper right corner of the graph screen indicates which of the function graphs the cursor is located on (that is, 1 is displayed for Y_1, 2 for Y_2, etc.).

Step 4   Press **left** or **right cursor** key (as required) to move the cursor to the desired point (this will become the new center of the viewing window).

Press ENTER to re-center the viewing window around the selected point.

Note: On the TI-83, the function rule is displayed at the top left of the screen when TRACE is on.

Using scaling/zooming options

Scaling is the process of changing the scales on either or both axes. Graphing utilities often refer to the process of zooming in and zooming out:

- **zooming in**—looking more closely at the graph through a smaller viewing window;
- **zooming out**—looking more widely at the graph through a larger viewing window.

Zooming in permits the user to focus more precisely on a portion of the graph. There are three possible ways to zoom in with the TI-82/83:

● Use the **Window** option to make the viewing window include a smaller region of the *X–Y* plane (see previous section).

● Use the **Zoom In** option to select a new viewing window center point and zoom in around that point.

● Use the **ZBox** option to select and zoom in to a "boxed" region within the current viewing window.

*The options available after pressing the **Zoom** key*

How to return to the default zoom level

Step 1   Press ZOOM .

Step 2   Press 6 to select the **6 : ZStandard** option (this will return to the default viewing window which is the region bounded by the points $-10 \le x \le 10$ and $-10 \le y \le 10$.

How to zoom in with the Zoom In option

The **Zoom In** option permits zooming in around a user definable coordinate. The TI-82/83 defaults to zooming in on both axes by a factor of four.

Step 1   Press ZOOM .

Step 2   Press 2 to select the **2 : Zoom In** option.

This takes you back to the graph screen. A cursor will be flashing (possibly at the origin). If you wish to zoom in around the origin, press the **ENTER** key without changing the cursor location. If you wish to zoom in around another point in the current viewing window, follow steps 3 and 4 below.

Step 3   Move the **cursor** keys to change the point around which the **Zoom In** will occur.

Step 4   When you have located the cursor in the region of interest, press ENTER .

Step 5   To zoom in further, repeat steps 3 and 4.

How to box zoom with the ZBox option

The **ZBox** option permits zooming inside a user definable rectangular "box" of the current viewing window.

Step 1   Press ZOOM .

Step 2   Press 1 to select the **1 : ZBox** option.

This takes you back to the graph screen. A cursor will be flashing (possibly at the origin). You then use the cursor arrows to define the zoom in "box". Follow the procedure below.

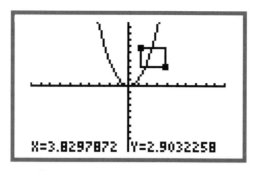

X=3.8297872 Y=2.9032258

Zooming in using the ZBox option. Note the box that has been defined

Step 3   Use the **cursor** keys to locate the upper left corner of the zoom box.

Step 4   Press ENTER.

Step 5   Use the **cursor** keys to locate the bottom right corner of the zoom box (a box will be created on screen).

Step 6   Press ENTER. (This then zooms into the boxed region.)

How to zoom out with the Zoom Out option

Zooming out permits the user to observe more of the graph, including perhaps more of the general shape or global features. The TI-82/83 defaults to zooming out on both axes by a factor of four. The **Zoom Out** option permits zooming out around a user definable coordinate.

Step 1   Press ZOOM.

Step 2   Press 3 to select the **3 : Zoom Out** option.

This takes you back to the graph screen. A cursor will be flashing (possibly at the origin). To zoom out from there, press the **ENTER** key without changing the cursor location. If you wish to zoom out around another point in the current viewing window, follow steps 3 and 4 below.

Step 3   Move the **cursor** keys to change the point around which the **Zoom Out** will occur.

Step 4   When you have located the cursor in the region of interest, press ENTER.

Step 5   To zoom out further, repeat steps 3 and 4.

How to use the ZPrevious option

The **ZPrevious** option permits the user to return to the previous zoom level. This is particularly useful if you have chosen an inappropriate viewing window, and wish to return to the previous viewing window you were using.

Step 1   Press ZOOM and then press the **right cursor** key to view the **Zoom Memory** options.

Step 2   Press 1 to select **1 : ZPrevious** to return to the previous zoom setting (or viewing Window).

How to use the ZInteger option

The **ZInteger** option permits the user to trace functions by redefining the viewing window so that each press of the **trace** cursor increments X (or Y) by 1 unit. This may be useful if you are considering integer only solutions to problems. This may also be useful if you are wishing to trace a function, incrementing by integer values of the independent variable, rather than incrementing by amounts dependent on the current zoom level.

Step 1   Press ZOOM .

Step 2   Press   8   to select the **8 : ZInteger** option.

Step 3   Move the **cursor** keys to select the center of the new viewing window.

Step 4   Press ENTER to re-plot the functions in the new viewing window. (This will also create axis markings at each 10 units.)

Step 5   Press TRACE to position the cursor on the relevant graph.

Step 6   Press the **right cursor** key to calculate the function value for successive integer values of the independent variable.

How to use the ZDecimal option

The **ZDecimal** option permits the user to trace functions by redefining the viewing window so that each press of the **trace** cursor increments X (or Y) by 0.1 of a unit. This may be useful if you are wishing to trace a function, incrementing by values of 0.1, rather than incrementing by amounts dependent on the current zoom level.

Step 1   Press ZOOM .

Step 2   Press   4   to select the **4 : ZDecimal** option. This will re-plot the functions in the new viewing window. The new viewing window has the dimensions $-4.7 \le x \le 4.7$ and $-3.1 \le y \le 3.1$. (This will also create axis markings at each unit.)

Step 3   Press TRACE to position the cursor on the relevant graph.

Step 4   Press the **right cursor** key to calculate the function value for successive increments of 0.1 in the independent variable.

How to use the ZSquare option

The **ZSquare** option attempts to display the true graph proportions by replotting the graphs of all entered functions with equal scales for the x- and y-axes. It does this by altering the current viewing window so that pressing the **left** or **right** cursor key moves the cursor the same distance as pressing the **up** or **down** cursor key.

Step 1   Press ZOOM .

Step 2   Press   5   to select the **5 : ZSquare** option. This will re-plot the functions in the new viewing window. (It will also create axis markings that have equivalent scale on each axis.)

How to change the zoom factors

The **default zoom factor** is four for each axis. This means that zooming in (or out) creates a change in the magnification of 400% in the direction of each axis. The procedure for changing any or all of these zoom factors is given below.

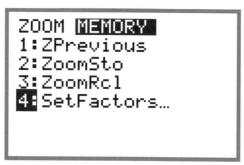

*The **SetFactors** option (for changing the zoom factors)*

Step 1   Press ZOOM .

Step 2   Press the **right cursor** key to move to the **Memory** option.

Step 3   Press   4   to select the **4 : SetFactors** option.

Step 4   Change the values of **XFact** or **YFact** as required.

Step 5   Press GRAPH to return to the graph screen.

WORKING WITH ADDITIONAL FEATURES ON THE TI-82/83

Creating a table of values

Creating a table of values from the function allows the user to observe another representation of the function. It could be a more convenient way of listing the function values of a number of functions at once. The example below is to create a table of values for the function $f(x) = x^2$ for $23 \leq x \leq 25$, with increments of 0.1.

How to create a table of values

*Setting the **Table setup** options*

Step 1   Press   Y=   and define the function $Y_1 = x^2$.

Step 2 Press **2nd** and then **WINDOW** for the **TblSet** key.

Step 3 Enter 23 as the new **TblMin** (or **TblStart** on the TI-83). This sets the new minimum *x* value for the table.

Step 4 Enter 0.1 as the new **ΔTbl** (*x* increment for the table).

Step 5 Select **Auto** as the data entry option for the **Indpnt** variable, and press **ENTER**.

This tells the TI-82/83 that you want the *x* values in the table generated automatically from **TblMin** (or **TblStart** on the TI-83)and **ΔTbl**.

Step 6 Select **Auto** as the data entry option for the **Depend** variable, and press **ENTER**.

This tells the TI-82/83 that you want the *y* values in the table generated automatically from the function rule and the *x* values obtained from the table.

Step 7 Press **2nd** and then press **GRAPH** for the **TABLE** key. The result is shown below.

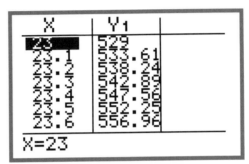

Sample table for f(x) = x² for 23 ≤ x ≤ 25 (for increments in the X values of 0.1).
*Use the **cursor** keys to scroll down through the list*

Plotting points

When attempting to fit functions to data that has been collected, it is convenient to plot data points, and then attempt to find function graphs which seem to line up with the points. The sample chart below illustrates a possible scenario where plotting points might be used.

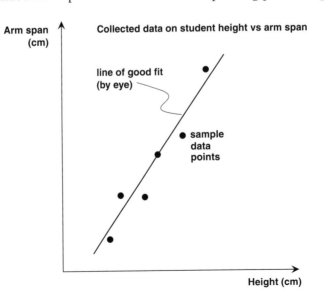

How to change the display precision

When entering data, it is useful to set the display precision first so that the data is displayed with the appropriate number of decimal points.

Step 1   Press MODE .

Step 2   Position the cursor on the second line of the **MODE** screen.

Step 3   Use the cursor keys to select a display precision of **0, 1, 2, 3, 4, 5, 6, 7, 8** or **9** decimal points, or **Float** to allow the TI-82/83 to select the display precision dependent on the figures entered and calculations performed.

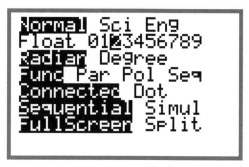

*Using the **Mode** screen to change the display precision*

How to plot points

In this example, use the following data values.

x	1	2	3	4	5	6
y	2.2	3.5	4.7	6.6	7.2	9.1

Step 1   Press STAT and then press   1   to select the **1 : Edit** option.

Step 2   If points are already listed in a column, you may clear them by moving the cursor to the head of the column (for example, **L1**) and pressing CLEAR then ENTER .

Step 3   Enter the *x* values in the table on the previous page into the column **L1**. Press ENTER after each entry.

Step 4   Enter the *y* values in the table on the previous page into the column **L2**. Press ENTER after each entry.

*Table of values for x and y shown in the **Stat** list screen*

Step 5   Press [2nd] and then [Y=] for the **STAT PLOT** key.

Step 6   Press [4] to select the **4 : PlotsOff** option. This returns the user to the Home

screen. Press [ENTER]. This clears all currently defined plots.

The Stat plots window—for defining statistical plot options

Step 7   Press [2nd] and then [Y=] for the **STAT PLOT** key.

Step 8   Press [1] to select the **1 : Plot1** option.

Step 9   Use the **cursor** keys and [ENTER] to set the options as shown in the diagram at the top
of the next page.

Setting statistical plot options for Plot 1

Note: On the TI-83:

● For **Xlist**, press [2nd] and [1] to select **L1**;

● For **Ylist**, press [2nd] and [2] to select **L2**.

Step 10   Press [Y=] and clear any entered function rules (so the statistical plot is clear).

Step 11   Press [ZOOM]. Then press [9] to select the **9 : ZoomStat** option. This will plot and
display the data points for **Plot1** in the new viewing window.

Step 12   Press [TRACE]. Using the **right** and **left cursor** keys allows you to observe the
coordinates of each point.

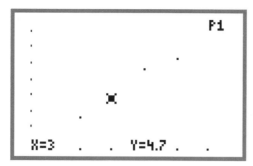

A scatter plot of the above data plotted on the TI-82/83 Graph screen

How to fit a function to data by eye

It is possible to try different functions that might fit the data points. One useful way of defining such functions is to denote the parameters of a function as letters. For this example (using the collected data above), we will try to fit a function of the form $y = Ax$, where A is the parameter that we will alter to try to achieve a good fit.

Step 1 Press Y= .

Step 2 To enter the parameter A, press ALPHA , followed by MATH for the **A** key.

Step 3 Press X,T,θ .

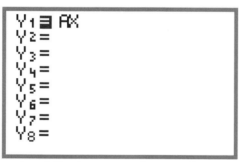

The Function definition screen showing the parameter A

Step 4 Press 2nd and MODE for **QUIT** to return to the home screen.

Step 5 To enter a specific value for A (for example, $A = 1.4$), press the following key sequence:

This sets the current value of the parameter **A** to 1.4.

The Home screen after parameter A has been set to 1.4

Step 6   Press GRAPH to observe whether the value of A has given a "good fit" for the data set.

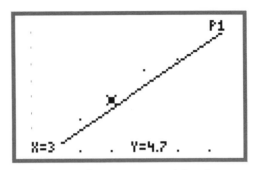

The Graph screen after parameter A has been set to 1.4

Step 7   Repeat steps 5 and 6 to improve the fit if necessary.

Note: Fitting a function to data by eye can be facilitated by using Split screen mode, which allows the user to view both the graph screen (at the top) and the home screen (at the bottom).

To access the Split screen mode, press MODE and select the **Split** (or **Horiz** on the TI-83) option.